AND THESE THREE REMAIN

an autobiography

DONALD MARK ODLAND

edited by Mark Patrick Odland

Xulon PRESS

WILMETTE PUBLIC LIBRARY
1242 WILMETTE AVENUE
WILMETTE, IL 60091
847-256-5025

721
Od4o

CONTENTS

———➤●◀———

PRELUDE

—————————

"Come to me, all you that are weary and are carrying heavy burdens, and I will give you rest. Take my yoke upon you, and learn from me; for I am gentle and humble in heart, and you will find rest for your souls. For my yoke is easy, and my burden is light."

(Matthew 11:28-30)

Dear Grandpa Don,

This autobiography is a blessing in so many ways. When I read your words, it's as if I can actually hear you speaking. I can hear the soothing tone of your voice and the quiet life in your laugh. When I read your words, it's as though you are with me, telling me an incredible story, the story of your life. There was so much I didn't know! So much I didn't expect. It's hard to believe that your thoughts and memories have been transferred from the typewriter to this beautifully published book, ready to be shared with the family who loves you so dearly.

Grandma Mary asked me to write this prelude to your book, and I'm so honored that I could play a small part in helping your story be heard. I never expected that I would tackle this large a project, but somehow it now makes sense. I see now that the timing was perfect. After graduating from Augustana College in December, I had the privilege of working as a lay pastor at a church in Sioux Falls for 3 months. When my job was finished, I still had 2 months left until the summer, and so I decided to use these months to focus completely on my creative gifts.

During that time I worked some on my art, but mostly on my poetry, poetry which I intended to publish someday.

As I researched various publishing companies for my book, I began to think about your autobiography. As summer drew near, the Lord laid on my heart how important it was to preserve your words for generations to come. I feared that if I didn't do something immediately, your story might sit on the shelf for years. I actually had the luxury of time, and so I decided to take action.

I removed your old manuscript from the glass case in your study room, snuck it out of the house, and hid it in my car. However, it was only a matter of time before Grandma Mary found out and became actively involved in the process. The following week I retyped your autobiography onto the computer. This allowed me to run it through spelling and grammar checks, divide it into paragraphs and chapters, give it a title, add some Bible verses, and edit it. Of course this was all done with the approval and input of Grandma Mary.

After editing your book, I feel even closer to you now. I feel like I know you so much better Grandpa. I wish you could have finished writing your story because I know there was so much more to tell. In fact, 40 years worth! And yet, somehow the abrupt ending to your book is graceful. As we read your last paragraph, we are left with an incredibly beautiful image. We are given a picture of you and Grandma Mary, young and full of life. There is an excitement in the air. The world is at your fingertips in a small town called Luverne. The place you would live, laugh, and love for over 40 years. It is here in Luverne that you would build a successful medical practice from the ground up and raise a loving family.

We all wish you could have finished writing your story Grandpa. But ultimately, simple words could never fully describe the impact your life has had on others. For those you have touched, no written record is needed. This 4th of July, amidst the campfires, pontoon parade, and fireworks, I saw something spectacular. I saw a large and loving family, a family that only exists because of the blessed love between you and Grandma Mary. You didn't finish your story with words Grandpa, but you finished it with actions. You finished it with love. And although you are no longer with us, the legacy you have given us is incredible. The title of your book seems very appropriate because you have left behind so much. Although you have passed away, faith, hope, and love remain.

We have faith Grandpa. Like you, we have faith in a God who is with us, who is by our side through all our joys and struggles. We have faith that He will give us peaceful hearts as we face the storms of this life without you. We also have hope. We hope for a bright future, praying that we would build meaningful and beautiful lives, pushing forward with optimism and excitement, just as you and Grandma Mary did so long ago. When I imagine you and Grandma Mary as newlyweds, I can't help but think of my beautiful wife Rachel, my partner in all and best friend.

Today, as Rachel and I begin to build our new life together at Luther Seminary, we now stand where you and Grandma Mary once stood. We continue where your book ended as the young couple facing the world together, hand in hand. There is so much beauty in this world, and so much life to live! And our lives are so much richer for having known you. We hope to see you again soon Grandpa. And it will be soon, for this life is but the blink of an eye. We will live lives full of hope, knowing with certainty, that because of Jesus, our Lord and Savior, we will one day see your face again. We also have love Grandpa, the greatest gift of all. We need not look far to see the love you have left behind. We see it every time we look in the eyes of family. The love given by you and Grandma Mary has been so selfless over the years and so full of grace. It has changed our lives forever.

The fragrant offering of your love continues to bloom

today in your children and grandchildren, and one day (perhaps soon) your great grandchildren! You have had such an impact on me Grandpa. I grew up knowing you as a kind and loving grandpa, but I now realize that you were so much more. You were a young man once, a little boy, and even a baby. You were a son, a husband, a father, an uncle, and a grandfather. You lived such an extraordinary life Grandpa, and I thank you for letting us share in your journey from the small boy you once were to the amazing young man you became. It is a treasure that we will always cherish. We love you Grandpa, and we'll see you soon. Your loving grandson,

Mark Patrick

CHAPTER 1

THE EARLY YEARS IN YANKTON

For it was you who formed my inward parts; you knit me together in my mother's womb. I praise you, for I am fearfully and wonderfully made. Wonderful are your works; that I know very well. My frame was not hidden from you, when I was being made in secret, intricately woven in the depths of the earth. Your eyes beheld my unformed substance. In your book were written all the days that were formed for me, when none of them as yet existed. How weighty to me are your thoughts, O God! How vast is the sum of them! I try to count them - they are more than the sand; I come to the end - I am still with you.

(Psalm 139:13-18)

I was born on October 23rd, 1926, named Donald Mark Odland, at Sacred Heart Hospital in Yankton, South Dakota. It was on a Saturday at 8:30 a.m. and I weighed 8 lbs. 8 and ½ oz. I was the 5th child of Ole Michael Odland and his wife, Clara Stensland Odland. I was also the 5th free child. My father was a pastor at Trinity Lutheran Church in Yankton, SD, but he was also a chaplain at the Sacred Heart Hospital at Yankton, SD. As a result of these endeavors, he was granted leniency fee-wise (financially) and there was no charge for my mother's prenatal care (such as it was in those days) or the hospital bill. She also had 4 additional deliveries there and a hysterectomy after I was born.

The doctor who delivered me was Dr. Hovde. I had later experiences with him and really liked the fellow, but of course when I was born I didn't know him too well. My mother had experienced a very difficult year because her mother died 6 months prior to my birth. Also, between that time and the time I was born, scarlet fever epidemics were prevalent and my sister, Maureen, had scarlet fever. At that time, with no antibiotics available, it was a very serious illness. As a result of the unknown cure for that disease, my father, as a pastor, was quarantined out of the house for 6 weeks and had to stay with the Snoens.

It is difficult to remember things in one's life prior to the age of 3 or 4, except under certain circumstances. Sometimes it's possible that the events that are repeated time and again in family circles make a person think that they can remember them themselves. I do have 2 events though, prior to the age of 3 and ½ or 4, that stand out very much in my mind. I think events such as this have to be so traumatic or big in one's recollection that they do stay with one. Two events took place when I was 2 years old. We took a trip to Wisconsin, (which was approximately a 450-mile drive) and you can imagine in those old cars, being crowded with 5 children and 2 adults! We stayed at a lake there, Lake Ripley, near Stoughton, Wisconsin, which was just south of Madison.

There was quite a group of people, with all relatives staying there. When we were leaving, they loaded up both cars (some of the relatives in one car and my family in another) and they took off, going to a nearby town named Cambridge, where my uncle Henry Thompson was a pastor. About halfway there, they decided to check because my mother was worried that I wasn't in the other car, and lo and behold, when they stopped the 2 cars, they found that I was not in either one, and I was only 2 years old! When they had broken all speed records getting back to the lake, they found me standing on the end of the dock talking to a lady. Now it's difficult for me to exactly remember all of that, but I seem to have a slight recollection of standing on that dock and being scared.

Another event I recall was a trip when I was 2 and ½ years old, going west in a '28 Nash car. We went west to the Black Hills where my father was presiding at a Bible Camp. The story is that one night we got stuck on the muddy roads and had to sleep (5 children and 2 adults) in the car overnight, and mother lost my shoes in the mud. That part I can't remember, but there was one thing that always stuck in my mind. We had stopped either coming or going and there was a rattlesnake that was dead along the road and they showed that to me. I guess I was quite impressed because I would have dreams about that for a long time.

The other thing that really stands out in my mind happened when I was about 3 years old. This shows that your mind is very impressionable when you are injured at that age (at the age of 3 or 4 or even younger). We lived in a house with 4 bedrooms upstairs and a bathroom upstairs. There was a bathroom in the basement as well, but the only bathtub was on the second floor. There was no water heater in those days, so you had to heat the water and pour it into a pail. Then you had to carry it upstairs after it was really hot and add to the cold water in the bathtub to get the right temperature. My mother was in the bedroom on the first floor, and she had heated this large kettle of water. I was running through the bedroom to find her and I stepped right into this nearly boiling water!

She said it was a large kettle with an open top. Of course, I let out a scream and hurt terribly and they had to have a doctor see me. I sustained 3rd degree burn around the right ankle. The thing that saved my foot was that I had a tight high-top shoe on. I can't remember Dr. Hovde coming to the house and making house calls. I had the front upstairs bedroom and that's where I laid for probably 4 to 6 weeks while they dressed it every other day or so. Every time they had to take the dressings off I would scream and holler because of the pain. In those days, the dressings had to be soaked and gradually pulled off because they didn't have such a thing as adaptic or telfa. To this day, I have that scar on my right ankle. It's never really bothered me, and in those days they didn't skin graft, so they let it heal over a period of 4 to 6 weeks.

As I mentioned before, I was the youngest of 5 children in the Ole Odland family. My older sister, Maureen, was almost 8 years old. My sister, Eunice, was 7 years old. I was the tail-ender or the so-called baby of the family. At the time

I was born, my Grandma Amanda Stensland (my mother's mother) had just died. Mother took in my grandfather (her father), Peter Stensland. He had a room upstairs all by himself, which caused some cramping of our family, as far as space is concerned. He lived with us for 14 years. Apparently, I was his favorite, being the youngest. My Grandfather Stensland was already 74 years old.

I'm sure that during the preschool era of my life I would follow the family around to different religious events. My dad, at that time, was a pastor at the Trinity Lutheran Church in Yankton, which was next door to the parsonage. Also, he was a pastor at the Elam Lutheran Church, 25 miles north of Yankton. We would go out there on Sundays and go to church. Of course, you always had your dad to listen to, and I had to be quiet and sit in the pulpit, especially in the town church where Mother was choir director. She would sit with me for a while and then she would leave to go up and direct the choir, and then come back and sit with me. I suppose I would tag along, too, with the older brothers on so many little escapades as a 2 or 3 year old. Apparently my mother was so busy that she didn't know where I was half the time.

I was about 4 years old when my brothers had built a little house out of wood and some tin roof, and I fell and cut my knee pretty bad. Also about that time, I had measles and was very sick for a while. I can remember lying in the downstairs bedroom feeling quite ill. About that time, some people moved in next door north of our parsonage and I met a little girl. She was my first girlfriend, apparently. Her name was Claudia. I did have some pictures at one time showing me bringing her home to show Mother. Then they moved out and a Methodist pastor moved in across the street, and he had 3 daughters (Susan, Mary, and Josephine Kerton).

Josephine was my age and somehow we became acquainted across the street and became good friends. I guess, according to my mother, I brought her in the house one day and said, "Well Mom, this is her." I remember one thing about that family, and that is that Josephine told me she was going to have her tonsils out. Not in those words, of course, at that age, but I remember going over to their house the day of the tonsillectomies, 3 of them. All 3 daughters were taken out in the kitchen and put on the kitchen table and their tonsils were taken out. For some reason, I was able to get in the house, nosey as I am, and was able to see the 3 daughters postoperatively, very soon after the operations. This was very disconcerting to me. Within a short time, they moved away to Wessington Springs, SD. To say the least, at that age, I was devastated. Of course, I had boy friends, too, at that age.

In the fall of 1930, just under the age of 4, I entered into Webster School in the Kindergarten class. The Webster School was located 1 block east and ½ block south on Mulberry Street. There were several of these schools in Yankton and I attended there my Kindergarten, 1st, 2nd, and 3rd grades. During that time, I became acquainted with a Danforth boy, Robert Danforth. He lived 2 or 3 blocks away and I can remember going to his house. His father was dead and his mother was living, but had suffered from tuberculosis and wasn't too well. The house was very large and seemed quite dark to me, but very beautiful inside. He had many toys that I didn't have or couldn't afford to have. Another friend I had was a boy named Carlton Kenyon. Carlton also had rather rich parents. He had many toys and a large train set up, and we played many hours there. Another boy, that I kept company with mostly, was Butch Anderson. I never did figure out what his first name was.

At an early age, I was very intensely interested in athletics, and especially football. At the age of 5 or 6, I was continually listening to games that Notre Dame, Iowa, and Minnesota would play over the radio. When I listened to the games, Nile Kinnick from Iowa was one of my heroes, later killed in World War II, and the present stadium is named after him, Kinnick Stadium. My heroes at Minnesota University were Sonny Frank, Bronco Nagurski, and Bruce Smith. Butch Anderson's oldest brother was a varsity member of the Iowa Hawkeye team and he gave us an auto-graphed football to play football with!

We played football every weekend over at Carlton Kenyon's empty lot next to his house. We had it lined up with yard markers and everything, like a real football field. I'm sure the lot wasn't that big, but to us it was a big field. We also would go over in the evening with my brothers and other friends and play games like Pump, Pump, Pull-Away and Hide and Seek, but the main game was Kick the Can. We had great fun doing these things. Of course, in those days, there was no television to distract your mind and also no Nintendo to fill your hours.

There was a presidential election, which was my first venture into politics, and this was held in 1932. The teacher talked to my mother at one of the PTA meetings. I was in 2nd grade then and I believe my teacher's name was Mrs. Larson. She told my mother, and I somewhat remember some of this too, that I campaigned in the class for President Hoover to get a second term. They had an election in the 2nd grade and I lost to Franklin Roosevelt, who later became president in that election. So, that was my first baptism into the political world. Now, why was I Republican at that age? It's difficult to say. Apparently it's quite environmental, because my mother was a very strong Republican. Of course, I was upset when I heard that President Roosevelt won, but my father was loyal American and he emphasized to me at an early age that no matter who gets elected, you have to be loyal to them, because they now were to be the President of the United States.

At home during those early years, we had a very close family of 5 children, our parents, and Grandpa Stensland.

Many evenings, we would make popcorn and sit around and tell stories, and I would play Crockinow and Rook with my grandpa. Also, at an early age, probably the age of 5, my Grandfather Stensland would take me down to the railroad depot, which was approximately 3 blocks north of our house. We would go down there hand in hand and he would talk to the depot manager and I would play around with the wooden carts with big wheels that were used to haul baggage off of the trains. I became very interested in trains, as I'll tell you later on. We would watch the freight trains and the passenger trains come in and out. He would also take me down to the watering station, where they would pick up water for the boiler and the coal for the burners.

There was a vacant lot between Trinity Lutheran Church and the next-door neighbors. I forgot their names now, but we sort of battled with them a little, with their kids. But we did get together a lot of times and played softball in the empty lot between the church and their house (that was east of the church). In the process, one of my brothers hit a softball and broke one of the church windows and my father had to report that to the Board of Trustees. Around that time (at the age of about 5) I tried to learn how to roller-skate. I did a fairly good job, and we roller-skated in the church basement when it was empty. I think one day we marked up the floor pretty good with roller-skates. That caused a few raised eyebrows, too.

The big Sunday event would be when church was over. Everybody raced home to get the Sunday newspaper and look at the "funnies." My favorites were the Katzenjammer Kids, Dick Tracy, Little Orphan Annie, and so forth. Also, there was a large lot across the street south of the church that was the Catholic playground. Sometimes we were able to go over there and play. I think my dad was very liberal-minded as far as different religions were concerned and he taught us to respect other religions and be proud of our own.

My mother was also supportive of my entertainment, as long as I stayed out of trouble. When I was in 3rd grade, one time I asked her if I could go to the show and she said, "You be sure to be home at 9:00." I went downtown and I can remember going to the show, a cowboy movie, at the Moon Theatre. This was a black and white cowboy movie and I liked it so well I stayed for the second show all alone. It was about 11:00 or 11:30, and they were ready to call the police when I showed up at home.

My father was very well liked as a minister in Yankton. At that time the head man at the WNAX radio station was named D.B. Gurney. He wanted somebody to preach on the radio, so he toured the city without anybody knowing. After he had listened to about 4 or 5 pastors in the city preach, he picked Dad to be the minister at the radio station, WNAX. As a result of this, every Sunday night there was a broadcast at approximately 8:00 from WNAX, sponsored by the station, and free, as my father didn't have to pay for the hour-long ceremony. He preached a sermon and we had the local choir and different soloists perform there. I remember sitting at home during 3rd grade and listening to the radio broadcast with my grandpa when we were playing games. My Grandpa Stensland was my babysitter and my protector.

In the fall of 1934, as I entered 4th grade, I transferred to another school called Garfield School. It was approximately 3 blocks west of our parsonage. We usually took the river route to the school along the river that was near our parsonage. On the way to and from school we could stop at a little store called Apstead's and pick up some candy and so forth whenever we wanted it or could afford it. My 4th grade teacher was Mrs. Thomas. I will certainly remember her because she is the one who switched me from being left-handed to right-handed, and every time I would write with my left hand she would call me in front of the whole class and yell out, "Donald, change hands!" And that's how I became right-handed as far as writing is concerned.

My interests were very much directed toward sports at this time and I would go with some of my friends and we would sneak into the Yankton College football games by burrowing under the fence. Many times we would be kicked out, but we would find another hole to go through because we couldn't afford the tickets. These years were during the depth of the depression in the United States and it hit Yankton and the crops around Yankton very hard. We were at the upper edge of the dust bowl and many times when we would travel to the church service and come back, Mother would get so disgusted because dust had infiltrated through all the windows and she would have to start housecleaning again.

I could see that things were getting pretty bad financially because when my father started at Yankton as a pastor, his salary was $100.00 a month, and then during the middle 20's, they raised it to $150.00, but when the stock market crashed in 1929 they lowered it again because of the depression. So, with 5 children, his salary was $100.00 a month. When I was in the 4th grade, a lot of times I would have to go down and get some groceries on my bike and always would have to give some excuse why we didn't pay our bill. They would charge it in large amounts and many times I would see my mother and father trying to figure out what to do because they would be 3 months behind on grocery bills.

About that time, I would follow my brother Paul, who was 4 years older, around on his paper route and help him deliver the Yankton Press & Dakota Paper. My 2 brothers had bicycles but they were stolen, so then we had to walk the whole route. First we walked downtown to get the papers and then delivered them. As a reward for my efforts, Paul would often give me a Popsicle or Fudgsicle, which cost a nickel at that time. Also, about that time, I was able to sell some papers myself, but these were 2 and 3 day old papers. I would take them around and sell them to people and sometimes they would feel sorry for me and give me some money, a few pennies or a nickel or dime for an old paper, just to get me out of their hair. Of course, that got back to my mother and father and they certainly stopped that in a hurry.

I was so intensely interested in sports, whenever I could I would go to the Central Grade School gym in the basement, and we would play there. We also had a basket at home down in the basement and would invite a lot of kids in and have parties with popcorn and so forth and have little tournaments with a rim that we played basketball around and chose up teams and so forth. Because there was no television, after school we'd hurry back home to hear a couple of radio programs that were on every day, such as Jack Armstrong, The All-American Boy, and Little Orphan Annie. These were the serials that were on every day, 5 days a week.

As I got a little older, I would follow my brothers and sisters out on hikes to the Chalkstone Cave, which was probably 3 miles out of town on the west side. We would hike through Sister's Grove next to Sacred Heart Hospital and down over the banks of the Missouri River to the large chalkstone cave that was there. We would play in there, write our names on the wall, and so forth, and then play down on the banks of the Missouri River. We were warned to stay away because of quick sand and we luckily never got into it. We would walk along the sand beach, pick up driftwood, and be real proud if we could find a piece of driftwood that looked like a cigar. Then somebody would bring along matches and we would smoke a little driftwood. This was my first experience with smoking. I suppose at the time I was 8 years old.

We would continue hiking sometimes out to the old cement factory west of Yankton, probably up to 5 miles away. There we would climb around on the buildings, which were dilapidated. I remember climbing up in a smokestack there. These smokestacks were giant, and of course had been abandoned for years. I suppose I climbed up in the inside of the smokestack on the metal rails (probably 50 ft.) and then looked down, got almost dizzy, and then climbed down. I never did that again. I also tried to attend as many high school basketball games as I could. Many times I went with my older brothers as well as by myself and with friends. You had to pay a small amount to get in, maybe a dime, and I was really a very loyal supporter of Yankton High School.

I had gradually become separated from some of my earlier friends, and being in a different school, I developed other friendships with Roland Mandini and Bill Johansson. Some of the girls I was friends with were Shirley Bittner and Luanne Miller. Also, about that time, my brothers and I, especially Paul and I, again went out north of Yankton to where they were building U.S. Highway 81 (It's still there). I suppose we must've walked 4 miles. We carried pails with us and picked up any extra cement that we could from the cement crews and carry it back, which was quite heavy. Then we would build roads around the trees in the back yard, using cement and sand. These were little roads, approximately 4-5 inches wide, but at our age seemed like nice big roads. They hardened, and we used them for trucks and little cars to go around the trees.

About that time, also the grasshopper scourge was in its full swing and some of the roads that we had had to be destroyed in favor of putting trenches around all of our trees. My father would do this and then dig the trench, and pile the dirt out a little ways. He would build a little mound around the trees and then put out poison for the grasshoppers because they were eating all the bark off the trees and destroying them. This was very, very successful, and the grasshoppers were dying by the hundreds. We would even collect grasshoppers, put them in little boxes, and then burn them (sort of a cruel way to do it). We always had a big garden in the back but it was very unsuccessful because the grasshoppers would come in and eat all the corn and carrots and beets and peas, right down to the ground.

I went downtown a couple of times during the summer between 3rd and 4th grade and 4th and 5th grade, and watched the bread lines at the WPA office where people were being fed that couldn't afford any food. Our family was in such tough shape financially that Dad's congregation in Elam put on a Labor Day celebration, and all the funds raised went to my father and the family. I'm sure it wasn't much, but it certainly helped. Farmers would bring in cream and butter and corn and potatoes and would help out the family that way. At this big celebration they would have food and recreation, baseball games, sack races, and races in general, and all kinds of athletic events to help raise money for the congregation. I enjoyed being in a pastor's family, especially at that age, because I got to go to a lot of things because of my father's status. People generally did look up to the pastor's family, as well as doctor's and dentist's families, and the mayor's family and so forth.

My 2 older sisters got to take piano from Mrs. Crockett, the mayor's wife. I envied them. I wanted to take piano lessons because I was quite musically inclined, but the money just ran out. Then, Mrs. Crocket died suddenly and that took care of that. In the meantime, my sister Maureen became very good at piano and so did Eunice, but Maureen especially. She entered into the high school music contest and lost out a close one to Joyce Steinbeck (Joyce was later queen at Augustana College).

My father would take me, being the youngest, on trips to a place out in the country west of Yankton, approximately 30 miles, at his own expense. Here he had some small services about every 2nd or 3rd Sunday, and I'm not sure what they called the congregation, but they formed it there. I would sit and listen to him preach and sing the songs with the people (probably 30-50 people would show up), and then we would come back and maybe they would take up an offering to help his expenses. Almost every Sunday we would go to the Elam congregation, where the salary there was very negligible. During the trip we would cross the James River in the valley north of Yankton on Highway 81, and met a lot of nice people out there. We would also go to evening services there, and I can remember the hymn sings and so forth that were very inspirational. I met a lot of nice young people there and we would go to ice cream socials and that was a lot of fun, too, especially the food.

When I was in 4th grade, in the back of our parsonage there was a little valley and a small gravel street. One day when I was walking down there, there was a garage and I opened the door to it. This is where I sometimes met some of my classmates. In the garage there were a couple of older men, and one of my friends was there too. He told me to go over there and meet these guys, which I did. They had a bottle with them and they were drinking out of this bottle of hooch. They called it hooch. I saw on the bottle it said "Whiskey" and I had heard a lot about that at home. They said, "Just take one taste of it," and that was my first taste of whiskey. I swallowed just a little, probably ½ teaspoon, and I got a little dizzy from it. I certainly almost threw up because I hated the taste of it. It was very strong.

About that time, I met a boy across the street, Keith Eide, and we played along a small river, which came right through the center of town and eventually joins the James River, which ran into the Missouri River east of town. We would fish in the stream, but there was hardly anything but bullheads in it. We also played there because there were some tall weeds, and we made huts and trails and so forth.

We thought we were big time African Hunters.

Our parsonage was located on Capital Street, running north and south, facing west, and the address was 606 North Capital Street, Yankton, South Dakota. About that time I was in 4th grade going into 5th grade, and I started on the mellophone. We rented a mellophone downtown and started on this, and my brother Paul started on a trombone. My sister Eunice was playing the bass violin in the high school orchestra, Maureen was playing a clarinet, and my brother Olin played the sousaphone. I was very proud of my older brothers and sisters, as they were very active in high school.

When I got lessons on the mellophone, I progressed quite rapidly and my father asked me to play over the radio. I did that at probably the age of 9. The song I played was "Holy, Holy, Holy." That was my first audition for Lawrence Welk. I'll have to explain myself at this stage that Lawrence Welk and his orchestra, which was in its infancy, played on WNAX every week, too, and they followed our church program. Many times, he would be sitting out in the audience and then would progress to the studio, which was glassed-in, and then his orchestra would play their program.

On Sunday, most likely in 1936, I was able to go with my parents up to Banton Park. This was a park that was developed on the west side of Yankton and owned and operated by Dr. Banton, a dentist. His home was next to the park, and it had a moat around it that had goldfish in it. I was really impressed with this. That particular Sunday afternoon I remember well. There were some pictures taken that I have misplaced for the time being, but several things happened that day. The first memory was that I was able to go and get some Juicy Fruit gum from the Lawrence Welk Orchestra, which was located in the park where they were playing that afternoon. Also, Leo Terry was there with his orchestra. It was some kind of a big celebration going on.

We had a separate gathering of church people and this

was at the west side of the park. We saw an airplane flying around and we didn't think too much about it, but then the rumor spread that there had been a crash. I went with my father to the crash site, which was located east of Yankton in a cornfield, and we were able to get pretty close to it. By the time we got there, they had extricated the two men that had died in the crash. Because my mother sang a lot of solos, she was often asked to sing at funerals. I would sit in the back and listen to her sing and sort of got involved a little that way. Sometimes the choir would sing. She was an alto soloist and at one time had sung solos in the St. Olaf Choir, which she only attended for a short time. She had to quit at St. Olaf after less than a year because of hepatitis.

During that summer, I also heard there was a car accident and so I rushed over to it (which was located a couple of blocks west of our home), and lo and behold, there laid a young fellow who apparently was later on identified as Olhauser. I forget his first name. He was a junior or senior in high school and had been riding on the fender of a car. He had been shaken off during some reckless driving and the car ran over him. There were a bunch of high school kids involved. He was lying along the curb and that's the first time I really saw a dead person who was recently killed. He had pools of blood in both eye sockets and this was quite an impression on me. I'll never forget that.

I really enjoyed singing as a young person, even in the Sunday school and at school. At Christmas time, in 4th grade, I was picked to be Joseph with the pageant for 3rd, 4th, and 5th graders, concerning the story of the birth of Jesus at Christmas. This was produced at the high school auditorium on the stage. I became very proud of that particular thing. This was a progression upward from the previous Christmas, at which time I was the innkeeper. My famous phrase was "There is no room for you in the inn." That brought the house down. But I took my job as Joseph very seriously and was able to come through with flying colors. I really didn't have to say too much, I just acted it out.

All this time in the 3rd, 4th, and 5th grades, I was witnessing my older sisters going through high school and their various activities, and I attended some of the concerts and sort of became involved with that also. On one occasion, my brother and I had rigged up a set-up so we could keep track of one of my sisters. She had a college boyfriend and she was a junior or senior in high school, and they were sitting on the davenport. I was hiding behind the davenport and I had a telegraph thing that I would use to telegraph up to my brother as to what was happening. I'm sure we were very much of a nuisance to our sisters.

My sister Maureen graduated from Yankton High School in 1936, and then attended Augustana College, so we started going up there for different things. In the fall of 1936, I was a 5th grader fully entrenched into the system of education in Yankton, and was very loyal to the system. We had a 5th grade basketball team and really had a lot of fun, plus trying to learn things, and by now I was a pretty accomplished right-hander. Although, I could play basketball with either hand and I was proud of that. I was really ambidextrous, you might say. I would eat with my left hand and write with my right hand, and my brain apparently got accustomed to the changes. By then, my father and mother thought I was pretty good at singing, so they also had me sing over the radio on a Sunday night with the church service.

We attended a lot of family reunions. My father was very loyal to his family, which consisted of 8 brothers and 3 sisters (a total of 11 children). I never really knew my Grandmother Stensland because she died before I was born, of course. My Grandma Odland died at a young age after having 11 children, and my Grandpa Erik Odland died in the year of 1932. The only thing I can remember about Grandpa Odland is that he came to our house, and apparently, about that time he had been sick. I remember him being very feeble and weak, and staying in our upstairs bedroom. So at that time, we had 2 grandpas in the house.

Our house in Yankton in those early years was more or less a hotel. At one time we had the Granskous, including Clemens, Ella (who is Dad's sister), and their 3 children. In fact, David Granskou was born in Yankton. After they had been expelled by the Communist guerillas in China where he was a missionary, they stayed at our house. Also, my uncle John Odland and his family stayed at our house at one time before they went to North Dakota to homestead. My uncle John Stensland stayed with us for a while as well. Also, my uncle Ben Stensland went to college at Yankton College. Before that, he went to Yankton High School and stayed at our house. So, you can see Mother really had her hands full with all those people in addition to her church work.

Many of our vacations turned out to be visits to Bible Camps. However, we did go to Wisconsin twice more and I can't remember the exact dates, but I remember playing at the Henry Thompson home in Stoughton, Wisconsin, out on the farm. We attended the Swan Lake Bible Camp one summer, probably when I was in 3rd grade. These were mostly in the summer of 1935. Finally, my dad was able to finance a new car. Up to that time, he drove a 1928 Nash. In the summer of 1935, we went to the Black Hills, where my father was dean of a Bible Camp near Paktola Dam. I road with my uncle, John Stensland, in his Pontiac, and my father with his '35 Dodge was able to take the rest of the family. That was a long trip in those days with 2-lane highways and some of them gravel and some of them paved. Also, we had to stop frequently because the cars in those days would heat up and boil over.

Between the spring and the fall of 1936, I met some new friends who I really was chumming around with a lot more. One was Johnny (I forget his last name), a black boy whose dad was a Methodist pastor in a black congregation. This was my first experience in learning how to cope with another race and I was encouraged by my father who was a friend of Johnny's father. I learned a little racial tolerance at that early age. Another good friend at that time was Roy Horlyck. Roy took me on some different escapades and I don't blame him because I certainly went along with him.

Our favorite haunt was the turnstile where the railroad engines would turn around. We also ran across the railroad bridges with our B-B guns and would shoot at different things. We also would sit down with some of the hobos who had gotten off the trains and listen to their stories as we sat around the campfires and so forth. I would never think that would be wise in this present day and age, but at that time it seemed perfectly safe, especially since my mother didn't know where I was. Another little hobby of ours would be to go down to the Milwaukee Railroad Depot, and mind you, I was 9 years going on 10 years old. This is where my grandpa used to take me when I was smaller. We would sneak around, hop on freight trains, and ride down to the watering station. It was a total of about 6 blocks or ½ mile and we felt very confident that the train would stop at that time. We would either sit on the boxcars or even sit on top of them if we could get away with it. We were constantly in the hair of the railroad workers and they were chasing us out more times than not. Again, this was dangerous, but children at this age seem to have no fear until they are injured.

Therefore, the fall of 1936 came and my sister Maureen was at Augustana College. My other sister, Eunice, was a senior at Yankton High School. My brother Olin was on the Yankton High School football team as a sophomore, and my brother Paul was a middle-semester 9th grader. I bring this all up because in the fall of 1936, probably around October, my father received a call from Dell Rapids, South Dakota, Lutheran congregation, to move there. This was quite upsetting to us children, who had been long-term residents of Yankton. We liked it there, we liked the house we were in, and enjoyed the congregation and so forth. I believe the first call he had from Dell Rapids was turned down. He had turned down previous calls from Mitchell, South Dakota, and River Falls, Wisconsin. I believe there were a couple of other calls, but we never found out about them.

My father was very respected in the Yankton community and he was still broadcasting over the radio and handling 3 congregations (One west of town, Elam congregation north of town, and Trinity Lutheran in Yankton). Then he received a second call from Dell Rapids to go there. It was a smaller congregation, and of course he prayerfully considered this call the second time, and then accepted the call. So, as a result, I would be leaving in the middle of the year before Christmas, and I temporarily stayed at the Granskou's residence in Sioux Falls. I stayed there because my cousin David was about my same age and we played together.

The 1935 winter and 1936 winter were very hard winters as far as snowfall and cold weather, and the winters of 1936 and '37 were particularly hard. About the time we left Yankton, the snow was car-high along Highway 81 (north of Yankton) and 1 lane wide, and was really a problem. Prior to the construction of the dams on the Missouri River, which was much later, the Missouri River had a tendency to flood every year. We had some really terrible floods in the Yankton area and my father would take me out in the springtime and we would watch the people marooned on the tops of their houses and the boats going to get them. So, at the end of December 1936, we moved to Dell Rapids, South Dakota.

CHAPTER 2

GROWING UP IN DELL RAPIDS

"Therefore I tell you, do not worry about your life, what you will eat or what you will drink, or about your body, what you will wear. Is not life more than food, and the body more than clothing? Look at the birds of the air; they neither sow nor reap nor gather into barns, and yet your heavenly Father feeds them. Are you not of more value than they? And can any of you by worrying add a single hour to your span of life? And why do you worry about clothing? Consider the lilies of the field, how they grow; they neither toil nor spin, yet I tell you, even Solomon in all his glory was not clothed like one of these. But if God so clothes the grass of the field, which is alive today and tomorrow is thrown into the oven, will he not much more clothe you - you of little faith? Therefore do not worry, saying 'What will we eat?' or 'What will we drink?' or 'What will we wear?' For it is the Gentiles who strive for all these things; and indeed your heavenly Father knows that you need all these things. But strive first for the kingdom of God and his righteousness, and all these things will be given to you as well. So do not worry about tomorrow, for tomorrow will bring about worries of its own. Today's trouble is enough for today."

(Matthew 6:25-34)

———⟫●⟪———

N ew Years Eve, 1936. The family was already located at
Dell Rapids, in the parsonage, but I was still at the
Granskou house in Sioux Falls. Several of us, including
David Granskou, Evelyn, and Ruth, were playing
Monopoly, when all of a sudden there was a terrible explosion. The force of the explosion was so severe that we
immediately went to the basement to see if the furnace blew
up. Then I ran next door to see if anything happened there
and they said that the staircase was separated from the
inside of the upstairs and downstairs. Downtown, all the
windows were broken out of Sioux Falls business places.
Windows were even broken in Dell Rapids.

Everybody was wondering if an oil storage depot had
blown up, but it wasn't too long before the mystery was
solved. There was a gang of thieves who had gathered at the
dynamite storage house just outside of Sioux Falls. They
had a fight, and in the fight, 2 or 3 of the thieves were in the
powder house. One of the thieves was able to cause this
explosion that rocked the countryside, and killed 2 or 3 of
the thieves with it. This was very impressive to me and was
in the news for several days with photographs.

So, that's the powder house sequence of events.
Following this, the next big thing for me was when we
moved to Dell Rapids. The first thing I noticed was that we

had moved from a very large 2-story house to a smaller 2-story house. During the time between the last pastor (who was Reverend Bringle) and the time that my dad came to Dell Rapids, the parsonage had a major fire. You could see evidence of it in the basement. All of the joints and joists were still charred. They had replaced some of it and covered a lot of it, but there was still that burnt smell down in the basement.

Instead of 5 bedrooms in Yankton, we moved to a 3-bedroom setup in Dell Rapids. I think that mother was initially very disappointed but gradually got used to it. The major problem was that Grandpa Peter Stensland had one room, which left 2 bedrooms for 5 children and 2 adults. The one upstairs bedroom was fairly good size and Olin, Paul and I were in 1 bedroom, on the back northwest side, upstairs. The other bedroom was Mother and Dad's, and there was one bathroom. My older 2 sisters had to sleep downstairs on the studio couch in my father's study. This was the way it was for the next 3 years until my grandfather Stensland died at the age of 88.

I, for one, can vouch for the fact that changing locations in the middle of the year was very difficult. It was difficult for me, being in 5th grade and having to get acquainted with a whole new set of friends when the cliques were already formed. But, it was doubly difficult for my sister, Eunice, who was the 2nd oldest. She was still living at home and had to leave in the middle of her senior year. I'm sure this was very difficult for her. As a result, Eunice lost out on some honors that she would have had in Yankton High School.

For the first month of January 1937, I was very homesick for Yankton and for my former friends, but through music (I still played the mellophone), basketball (I was playing on the 5th grade team), and also through church activities, I was able to get acquainted. My first friends that I got acquainted with were Alan and Gerald Tufteland, who lived a block away. We were in church together, too. I also met Donny and Robert Olson, of the Clarence Olson family, who lived 1 and ½ blocks away. The Olson family was very good to me and we used to go down there in the evenings and play cards. The name of the game was "Flinch." I had never heard of this game before. It was a lot of fun, especially with all the popcorn they made. The other games we played were Monopoly and we played that mostly over at the Tufteland's.

One advantage I had was that I came from a larger school, and when I came to Dell Rapids, I found myself considerably ahead scholastically. I was further along through my studies then Dell Rapids was. When I say this, I'm not downgrading the Dell Rapids educational system, but it just happened that way. I became a member of the grade school band and played mellophone, and was quite advanced already for my age. One of my good friends in the band was Vernyl Peterson, who was the 8th grade French horn player in the same band. Our director was B.G. Monk. He also had the high school band.

In May of 1937, my sister Eunice graduated from high school with honors and did real well in spite of losing some credits from transferring to Dell Rapids High School. By now, I was quite well acquainted and had several friends in Dell Rapids. We did many things together, especially with Alan Tufteland and Bob and Donny Olson. During the summer months of 1937, I recall exploring the Dells, which was intriguing to me. On one occasion, we were able to trap some crabs, which were small, and we used them for bait. Then we would fish for bullheads with the crabs. We did catch some carp and bullheads, all on our own, with very homemade equipment. In addition to this, I went fishing with my father. He loved to fish along a dam and in the Sioux River for bullheads, and up at Brandt Lake, near Chester, South Dakota, for walleyes.

Financially, we were a little better off than we were before, but not too much, and things were pretty tough. My sisters and brothers all worked. My brothers worked at Morell's and they had an old coupe that they drove back and forth in. I got a job working at "Doc" Malean's, a farm out north a few miles from Dell Rapids. Somebody would come and pick us up and we would go out there (a bunch of us 6th and 7th graders) and weed vegetable gardens for him. As I remember, he was quite a crude character. He chewed tobacco all the time and he would spit in our rows. Every once in a while you would get a handful of spit tobacco that would make you almost want to throw up.

This was a very difficult type of work. We had to work 8 to 10 hours on our hands and knees. He would come along all the time just like a custodian and would point out that we hadn't picked up a certain weed. We were weeding peas and radishes and carrots and beans and it was very difficult work. I would come home with my hands so stiff that I could hardly close them at the end of the day. Our knees got all scuffed up, too. Once in a while, you had to stand up and stretch, otherwise you would just go crazy with pain in your knees. This was all done for 50 lousy cents a day. 50 cents was 50 cents at that time, but we were way underpaid. He was taking advantage of child labor. All he would tell you was if you didn't like it quit, and he would get somebody else. Several did quit. I managed to stick it out for about 6 weeks.

There were other things to do in Dell Rapids as well. They had a beach on the river, heaven forbid, but that was better than nothing as far as swimming was concerned. There was sand on the beach and the water was quite muddy at times. I learned to swim quite well then. Initially, in Yankton, we did swim at the school, but one of the life-guards kept dunking me because I wouldn't go under water. I got tired of that and I quit swimming there. After I learned to swim, he didn't bother me as much. In Dell Rapids, I would go swimming quite a bit when I had the time. We would hike out to Mile Grove and Two-Mile Grove, which were 1 and 2 miles from Dell Rapids, hiking along the river. We also had summer grade school band. I was getting better all the time, and thinking about switching over to French horn in the fall.

In the fall of 1937, my sister Maureen was a sophomore at Augustana and my sister Eunice was a freshman at Augustana, which crimped the family budget considerably. Contrary to the opinion of a lot of people, the pastor's sons and daughters did not get any advantage over anybody else as far as finances were concerned. Things were just tight all over, especially with Grandpa living at our house. When Dad came to Dell Rapids, his salary was $90.00 a month at Willow Creek congregation (6 miles west of Dell Rapids) and I believe the salary in Dell Rapids was probably close to $200.00 a month at the most. The problem was, during the late depression years (1936-1937) Dell Rapids was not able to come up with the money all the time. The greatest offender was Willow Creek. They didn't pay him for at least 4 months before he finally got paid, and we ran up some bills again at different stores.

I used to go downtown and get the milk by a gallon pail. I can't remember exactly what the cost was, but I think a gallon of milk in those days ran probably 80-90 cents. I would walk 5 blocks downtown and back up the hills. Dell Rapids is a beautiful town and has a lot of hills, which were really nice during the winter months because we would slide down a big hill called Beto Hill. At times when the snow and ice was packed good, you could slide all the way to the Lutheran Church (2 blocks), and then turn and go 2 blocks down the other way. Of course, it would be a long way back, and uphill all the way.

In September, I started 6th grade. My teacher was Mrs. Frank Briley. In the early part of the year, for some reason I got teased a lot about being from Yankton, SD, where the "crazy" people were. My brother, Olin, told me to just tell them that in Yankton we locked them up and in Dell Rapids they let them run free. To my surprise, I was admitted to the high school band as a 6th grader because of my progress on the French horn. This meant that I could go with the band on trips also. We would take trips to Hobo Day and the University of South Dakota for Dakota Day and march in parades in the fall. I did practice a lot and got better all the time. Also, as far as music is concerned, I worked with my mother accompanying me singing, and also helping me with my voice. She also played for me when I played the French horn. I had several public appearances with the French horn, playing at women's clubs and church gatherings, both in Willow Creek and Dell Rapids.

In sixth grade, I had additional friends (Donald Bach, Orton Wagner, Dick Roth, and Alan Tufteland). As far as neighborhood friends, (Ora Jane, Mavis and Ardis Heeren, Georgia Merry, and Alan and Gerald Tufteland) we would play games in the fall outside, the usual games that we mentioned before. Once in a while, Mary Lou Thorson and Kay, her sister, and another girl I later would get to know better (a Mary Margaret Hermanson) would get together. There was a Joanne Martini that we played with also.

In the 5th and 6th grade, I didn't have any more alcohol to drink (Ha Ha!). My dad didn't ever know about that little episode previously mentioned when I was in the 4th grade. Dell Rapids was pretty much landlocked. We did have the Sioux River, but there was no driftwood along the Sioux River, so I gave up driftwood smoking (Just kidding! I didn't like the driftwood too well!). I learned a new habit from the Tufteland boys. We went out into the cornfield and in the fall of my 6th grade year we would pick up some dried corn silk out of the ears, wrap it up in toilet paper, and we had a little hut that we would smoke this in. It sounds like I was a real renegade, doesn't it? Well, pretty soon you would practically choke on it, so you couldn't smoke very much anyhow. It was just the idea you were doing something dumb and getting away with it.

I would get into trouble once in a while, and one day I can remember in the 6th grade, I was shooting a water hose at my brother and some of his friends and they picked me up and threw me in the lily pool. We had a little lily pool in the backyard of the Lutheran parsonage. It was only about a foot deep with goldfish in it and it had a little center area in it with water around the outside. They just threw me in! I didn't try to shoot them with water anymore after that. That taught me a lesson.

Of course, church and Sunday school meant a lot in our family. The family home was also a place where people would come and get married. My mother would play the piano for them and maybe my sisters or brothers would sing. I would sneak around the corner and watch the wedding from a distance. We also played ping-pong on the dining room table and sort of scratched it up a little, but that was a form of entertainment. We played football (sandlot type) in the fall. I always thought I'd be a great quarterback, but I never got the chance. During the winter months, I would not only play in the band, but we had a 6th grade basketball team, and we enjoyed playing basketball a lot. I continued to try and develop my expertise in basketball and other sports. At that age, I was so intense on playing basketball and practicing basketball, that we would clear off the driveway, which was gravel, and push the snow aside and play no matter what kind of weather it was.

We had a hoop and a bangboard on the edge of the garage and lights put up so we could play at night. Even in the very cold weather, without gloves, we would play. Doing this, we developed a lot of good eyes for shooting. This is the same group of classmates I played with all the way from 5th grade on up to seniors in high school, which accounted later in high school for tremendous success on the basketball court. One of my friends, Dale Dunn, had a barn on the edge of town, and we cleaned out the bales of hay and put up a basketball hoop so that when it was 0 degrees outside, we could play out in the barn. We would have tournaments every Saturday.

As far as other activities during the winter, during my 6th grade time of life, we would do a lot of sliding. We had a great hill to slide on, Beto Hill, named after a lady and family that lived halfway up the hill. This was a real steep hill, and at the bottom of the hill lived a Mrs. Chris Paulson. She would enjoy watching us come down the hill and slide in the evenings and mornings of vacation days. The city would block it off so it was safe for sliding. After all, the cars could hardly make it up that hill anyhow. That happened to be the hill that started at the top where the parsonage was.

By now, my brother Olin would be playing on the varsity basketball team and my brother Paul would be playing on the 10th grade team. Naturally, we went to all the games. My father was a rather intense fan. In those days, there were hardly any school buses and all transportation to basketball games had to be arranged through parents of the players. I don't think he ever missed one. In fact, sometimes if they played on Saturday night, he would be so hoarse he could hardly preach the next morning. Some of the parishioners complained that he yelled so loud and got so excited, but then he would tell them that the time for a prayer service is at church rather than at the basketball game. That seemed to shut some of them up.

After the games, even when my brothers were playing and when I was playing, my father would always go down in the locker room to congratulate them, win or lose, and they almost expected him. After all, Ole Odland, my father, was fullback at South Dakota State, and at that time it was called South Dakota Agriculture College. He was a starting fullback in his junior and senior year in 1912. We looked in his annual and it stated that "Ole Odland would rather play football than fuss." We asked him what "fuss" meant and he said, "Well, it's the same as necking nowadays."

My father was a graduate of South Dakota State at Brookings. In those days, they had to do a lot of fall work on the farm, which they do now, too, but they didn't have the machinery. They used threshing machines, run by steam engines. So he and his brothers took 5 years to go through college at South Dakota State because they could only start quite late and end early, but he was not in the theological courses at first. He graduated from South Dakota State as a civil engineer and then he met my mother and they decided that he would go into seminary and become a minister, and that's how he got started in that field.

The spring of the year was exciting because of District Basketball Tournaments. During those early years, Dell Rapids was dominated by Flandreau in high school basketball. Somebody said once, "When the Odlands came to town, that all changed." I don't quite agree with all of that, but I think things did change about that time because when my brother Olin was a junior and senior, they won the District Tournament at Dell Rapids High School. That was a big event. They went on to get beat in the Region Tournament. I witnessed a lot of those games and enjoyed them immensely. Also, in the spring of my 6th grade year, I was eligible to go to the music contests with the high school band. During that summer, the usual thing was swimming at the Sioux River, and although it was a very muddy river to swim in, they did cover the beach with sand, and tried to cover the river itself with sand, and it was quite wide. I was becoming a pretty good swimmer by then. The usual things took place as far as Bible camps and so forth. Also, we had a large garden to take care of and had to help with weeding. Both of my older brothers were working at Morrell's that summer and they had an old car, which was a Nash coupe, and we had a lot of fun with that.

In the fall of that same year, which I believe would be 1938, I entered the 7th grade. There was no such thing as junior and senior high then. It was just 8 grades and then you went to being a freshman, so I was closing the gap. My teacher was Mrs. Gladys Martini. I got along pretty good with her, although a lot of the kids didn't like her because she was so strict, but I think I learned a lot that year in math and so forth. When I look back on the latter years of grade school, I think foundations are so important in education, and I think I got a good foundation, even in a small school. We started playing more touch football and even tackle football during recess, and before and after school. There was no organized football. It was mostly pickup games where you chose your teammates. This could get pretty rough at times.

There was one boy in the class who seemed to bully everybody. His first name was Bob and his last name started with a "T." One day he really got bullyish and tore my shirt a little and we really went to it. Both of us had to stay after school, but he never bullied me or any of the other kids after that. At that particular time, I was getting taller and quite thin, but quite strong. In the evenings, we would play games in the neighborhoods. We would also play basketball under the lights in either Donny Bach's or our yard or out at the Dunn farm. One night we were going to get together with a bunch of kids (I think it was Doris Burg, Alan Tufteland, Bob Olson, and some others, including Mary Hermanson) and go down and get Joanne Martini (the daughter of my teacher) and all go out and play tag and so forth. We went to her house and they said she was gone to Sioux Falls with her mother. I remember that so distinctly because the next morning we found out that Joanne Martini, who was in the 8th grade, was killed on the way back from Sioux Falls where they had been shopping. They ran into another car at Midway, which is halfway between Sioux Falls and Dell Rapids on Highway 77. A couple of days later, I went to her funeral with a bunch of students and it was very sad. I'm sure Mrs. Martini was never quite the same after that.

Of course, I was in the band again with the same band director. When it came to later in the fall and early winter, we started basketball as a 7th grade basketball team and I must say that we really had a good team, because as 7th graders, we really took on all opponents of the same age group, (7th and 8th graders) and usually won. This was indeed a forecast of things to come, but at the time we didn't know it. By now, both of my sisters were in school at Augustana College and my oldest brother, Olin, was a senior in high school and going great guns in athletics, both in football (which was a winning season) and basketball, winning the District Tournament. Of course, our family didn't miss any of the games, especially because he was playing. He was Captain of the football team and as a younger brother, I was always around the locker rooms, and I got used to that locker room smell.

Paul, my next brother, who is 4 years older than I am, was now a junior in high school and competing to be the top-notch trombonist in the band. Olin played the sousaphone in the band and I played the French horn. That particular year, we won 1st place in the District Contest. That was a big thing. We played at the Grand Concert that they had in those days where the 1st place in anything would be the ones who played for that night at Madison, South Dakota, at the college. This was a really big event for a 7th grader. Also, that fall we went to the South Dakota State Fair by train. Before we went, we took a tour of Minnehaha County with the band during the late summer months. I can remember very well that we went to Sioux Falls and the Chamber of Commerce there treated us with free pop. It was the first time in my life I had ever gotten a chance to get any free pop. Believe it or not, I had 6 bottles in a row of orange pop. I was quite dehydrated to begin with, but I really got a sick stomach afterward.

We had recently received new uniforms and we were really proud of them. They were bright orange and black. We toured Garretson, Colton, Madison, Flandreau, and back to Sioux Falls, where we were in the parade. This was just before we went to the State Fair. They kept pretty good tabs on us at the State Fair, but we got to do some things and watch the races and so forth, and then we played a concert in front of the Grand Stand. I can remember taking the train back. We had to wait for one of the girls, Marilyn Martini. She sort of had a crush on my brother, Paul, at the time, but she was out with somebody else, and she didn't get on the train hardly in time, and we had to hold the train back because of that. That was the fall of 1938.

In the band, I was a member of the 4 French horns, trying to work my way up. At the time, I was in 4th chair, and Burgy was 1st horn; 2nd horn was a girl named Betty, and third horn was Vernyl Peterson. I was 4th horn, which wasn't bad for a 7th grader. I was playing more solos for church and going to different churches with my dad to play solos at the Willow Creek, East, and West Nidaros churches. During that year, too, we made many trips to Augustana to visit my sisters. They were living in a house called the Rud House, which was next to campus. My sister Maureen was in her 3rd year of college, and my sister Eunice was in her 2nd year of college. Both of them had switched to "2-year Normal" for teaching purposes. This was an acceptable type of teacher's certificate for 2 years of college, not only because of the shortage of teachers, but also because of the expense of college during the depression years. They planned to teach at that particular time. SO, in the spring of 1939, both of my sisters finished at Augustana and graduated from the 2-year program.

During that school year, I watched a lot of the Augustana football and basketball games. My father went to a lot of them because he was a strong supporter of Augustana College. He was also on the National Board of Education. Dad was a chairman of it at the Central Church in Minneapolis for the whole country. It was called the Board of Parish Education. He did go up there quite a bit, and he was also on the Board at the Bethesda Nursing Home, or "Home for the Aged" in Beresford, SD, and he would go to those meetings, too. Sometimes I would go along with him. My brother, Olin, worked as a lifeguard during that next summer. To get his lifesaving certificate and certificate for teaching swimming lessons, he and my father and I went to Minneapolis. This was the first time I ever went to Minneapolis, just finishing the 7th grade and after Olin graduated from high school.

During the summer of 1939, my brother Paul and I worked at Dyvig Nursery at Baltic, South Dakota. Some of the time, we had rides over and back. It was approximately 6 miles away as the crow flies and many times we had to walk to and from Baltic Nurseries, and usually took the route along the railroad track from Dell Rapids. We would sort of skip along and throw stones and so forth. A lot of times we would walk over there and then Dad would pick us up. We would work long days, 8-10 hours, weeding again, mostly vegetable gardens. There were quite a few there. It was much improved conditions over the summer before. Our wages were $1.15 a day, but if you worked real hard and did a lot of rows, you could get $1.35 a day. Also, I helped my brother with the Argus-Leader paper route during the year and later on had my own paper route with the Argus-Leader. We would bring the collections to Mrs.

Graves and she would dole out our salary, which was probably $2.00 a week. I always had the feeling that she was making a little money off of us, but I guess that was her prerogative.

During that summer I also helped my sister Eunice learn how to play French horn, baritone, and trumpet, because I knew the fingering for all three. She also tried to learn the clarinet from somebody else and the sousaphone from somebody else. The reason my sister Eunice had to learn these different instruments was that she was going to have a job at Wallace High School in Wallace, South Dakota. In fact, the job consisted of teaching the upper 4 grades and having the high school band. She played a bass violin instrument in the Augustana symphony.

Then came September 1st, 1939. Why is that so important? It is the time that Germany invaded Poland and it was officially the start of World War II, which would affect all of our families in the community eventually. I was starting 8th grade and went out for football with the high school team. Only about 3 or 4 of us bigger students went out for the varsity team. It was difficult because they were somewhat short on numbers in a smaller school like Dell Rapids, and we often got caught scrimmaging against the sophomores and juniors and came home with a lot of bumps and bruises. By now, my sister Eunice was teaching school at Wallace, South Dakota. My sister Maureen was engaged to John Muller, a local farmer, and spent a lot of time with him, of course. My brother, Olin, was of course, playing football as a freshman at Augustana and doing very well. My brother Paul was a senior at Dell Rapids High School and he was on the football team, so I was involved not only suiting up with the team but also watching him play and following games both at Augustana and Dell Rapids High School. We followed the news closely, hoping that the United States wouldn't get involved in the war in Europe.

In the fall of 1939, the National Corn Picking Contest came to Dell Rapids and was held about 3 or 4 miles north of town, I believe. In those days, the National Corn Picking Contest, which was by hand, was a big thing. In fact, they took several fields to use for concessions and it was a big celebration. Approximately 100,000 people showed up! The Dell Rapids High School band, of which I was a member, played a concert out at the corn-husking contest and also marched in a parade out there. The weather was rather cold, however, as I remember. I also sent out and helped clean up the area afterward and we got paid so much an hour to do this. The big movie that year that came out was "Gone with the Wind," and I saw it about 3 times. It was different from other movies because it was 4 hours long and they let out school one day for us to go. When we would go to the movies, we would see newsreels that would show pictures of the war in Europe. Of course, in 1936, the Japanese invaded China, so we had 2 areas of war to watch, and I was very interested in world events.

Thanksgiving and Christmas were always big events at our house and we would frequently attend family reunions, mostly at Hurley, South Dakota, and at Sioux Falls. Sometimes we would have a family reunion as a picnic in Sherman Park. During the winter months, I was on the 8th grade basketball team and we were developing into a real good team. We won most of our games, some by very large margins. We also would play against the 9th grade team and we would beat them frequently, and other schools, too. My coach and our 8th grade teacher was Norris Gomsrud. He had a habit of looking into the trophy case outside the 8th grade classroom and you could use it as a mirror to see what was going on in class when he would leave the room.

The big thing then was not shooting spit wads with rubber bands, but shooting lead foil. You could get lead foil wrapped around many things at the grocery store and so forth and take it up in little wads and use a rubber band to shoot it. I didn't really partake in this too much because I was afraid of really hurting somebody. If you would shoot somebody in the back of the neck, you could really cause a welt. They would do this during times when the teacher would leave the room. One day he caught 2 kids doing this and he made them stand up in front of the class and shoot each other full force in the chest. They had welts all over their chests and this was his form of punishment. Neither of them did this anymore after that.

As I said before, when we moved to Dell Rapids, we brought Grandpa Peter Stensland with us and he stayed in the house and occupied one of the bedrooms. By the time he left Yankton for Dell Rapids, he had been a member of our household for 10 years, since I was born, and would continue to stay with us. Mother took care of him for 14 years. The last 2 and ½ years, he was bedridden. He occupied the 2nd story bedroom on the northeast side. So, as a result, it cramped the family considerably, as described before. By this time, when I was in the 8th grade, he already had been bedridden for more than a year.

There were no rest homes in those days except for poor farms to put people in and they were substandard. Mother took good care of him. He was 87 when I was in 8th grade and turned 88 during my 8th grade time. The interesting thing is that he kept track of everything I did. He was sort of my godfather in a way. I would go by his room and he would always hit his cane on a can or hit the can against the table and that would be a signal for me to come and see him. He would always know when I played in a basketball game or football game and he wanted to know all about it, even though he didn't understand these games too well. At times, we would play Rook or card games. I learned at an early age it would be better to let him win more than half the time to keep him happy. He did have one habit that was very bad and that was chewing tobacco, especially as he became bedridden. He had to have mother clean up the spittoon, and she just hated this, but that seemed to be the only thing that kept him going. So, as a result, she would bring 3 meals a day up to him and give him baths and was very dedicated to helping her father.

My musical career continued. I sang in the grade school chorus, sang solos at different places, and played French horn solos at different places as well. I was improving all the time with the French horn. In the spring of 1940, toward the latter part of my 8th grade level, I was a member of the French horn quartet, consisting of Burgy Halvorson, Betty, Vernyl Peterson, and myself. We went to the District and received superior, and we played in the Grand Concert. Also, the band got superior, and the band was invited many places to play, and we also played in the Grand Concert. The French horn quartet was invited to come down to South Dakota University, which was my first big trip of this sort. During the fall of my 8th grade career, we went both to Hobo Day as well as Dakota Day (at the University of South Dakota) and had a real good time. That made quite an impression on me.

Back to the French horn quartet. We were invited to some kind of musical festival at South Dakota University in Vermillion, and I remember going out on the stage with the quartet and we were given a standing ovation. Of course, I continued to watch high school basketball and football because my brother Paul was playing. He was Captain of the basketball team and Captain of the football team, but he always lived in the shadow of his older brother Olin, who was quite a star in both athletic endeavors. Paul was a very good student and by now I had taken over his paper route with the Argus-Leader, and I got to know a lot of people around town because of it. Paul graduated from Dell Rapids High School in May of 1940 and he was salutatorian. We were very proud of him. He also won a superior in trombone solo. Valedictorian was Merrill Wicks. Our 8th grade basketball team went to the Tri-State Basketball Festival in Sioux Falls, and we won our division. We had a very cohesive unit.

During the summer between my 8th and 9th grade, I first of all was involved in the wedding of my sister, Maureen, who married John P. Muller on June 14th, 1940. During the summer months I then went out and worked at their farm. Although it was hard work, we still were better off than we were weeding gardens as we did 2 years before. I didn't do too much tractor work because I had never done it before, but I did do a little plowing. I certainly helped stack hay. I wasn't good enough to run the hayrack for bundles, but I did shock oats and barley and wheat. He had about 10 cows, which I milked by hand with his help, of course. I learned at that time why farmers have strong grips, at least at that time, because of their milking cows all the time. Maureen and Johnny lived in the second house south of Henry Muller's, his parents. I would stay at their house during the week and come into town on Saturday nights and Sundays. Saturday nights, we would usually go downtown and find some friends, etc. Saturday nights in those days were big celebration nights where all the farmers would come into town, get their groceries, and stay until all hours of the night. Also, people would go down to the Pavilion for dances.

During the spring of 1940, of course, France, Belgium, Holland, and Norway were all invaded by Germany, and Hitler reigned over almost all of Europe. This was starting to alarm a lot of us in this country, although at that time, President Franklin Roosevelt was starting to prepare us for war, but we were actually ill prepared, and most of the congressmen wanted to stay out of the war. At the same time, we didn't know Hitler was killing Jews. It was a very well kept secret to the world at large.

During the early part of the summer of 1940, I did take

time to go to the Bible camp at Lake Geneva in Alexandria, Minnesota. It was the first time I had been up there. My father was dean of the camp, and I worked in the kitchen. We would help serve the table and wash the dishes, and so forth. The main thing I remember is that we lived in tents and had a lot of fun running back and forth between them. I met a pastor's son from Starbuck, Minnesota, and the ones that went with me from Dell Rapids were Alverna Wilson, Lois Mormon, Morgan Christensen, Alan Tufteland, and Henry Wilson, amongst others. These were all classmates. I remember pouring coffee for one of the Luther League advisors and sort of poured some over her shoulders. It wasn't real hot, but that really taught me a lesson, too. She was, of course, not very happy with me. Whenever we would go to these Bible camps, my father would always get out there and play softball with the other pastors, and the pastors and the league advisors would play against the students. I remember one time he slid into 2nd base and ripped his pants, and everybody got such a kick out of that, that he was such a regular fellow.

CHAPTER 3

BECOMING A MAN

Love never ends. But as for prophesies, they will come to an end; as for tongues, they will cease; as for knowledge, it will come to an end. For we know only in part, and we prophesy only in part; but when the complete comes, the partial will come to an end. When I was a child, I spoke like a child, I thought like a child, I reasoned like a child; when I became an adult, I put an end to childish ways. For now we see in a mirror, dimly, but then we will see face to face. Now I know only in part; then I will know fully, even as I have been fully known. And now faith, hope, and love abide, these three; and the greatest of these is love.

(1 Corinthians 13:8-13)

I n the fall of 1940 I was a freshman in high school, and we had to wear green beanies for about a month. We were ridiculed quite a bit as freshmen until we had to finally take our beanies off at a high school bonfire. Also, as a freshman, I played on the football team. I was about 6 ft. at that time and about 150-160 lbs. They had me playing right guard. After a few games, I was able to start as a freshman. My sister and her husband lived out in the country. We would see them quite often. My sister Eunice was teaching at Wallace, South Dakota, as I mentioned before. My brother Olin was on the football team at Augustana and we went to all their games. These were played on the new field. They used to play on the old athletic field where the dormitories now are, but then they made a new field where the Union building is now. That was very beautiful.

By now, I had become quite a student. In 7th grade, I had half A's and half B's. In 8th grade, I had 2/3rds A's and 1/3rd B's. In 9th grade, I was really interested in science, but at the time I really thought I'd probably be a minister some day. As far as the high school band was concerned, now I had been in it 3 years, and challenged Vernyl Peterson. I became 1st chair and he became 2nd chair. As freshmen, this was quite an accomplishment! The other two older 1st and 2nd chairs of the horn section had graduated. By now, we had new band director, Mr. Wallender, because Mr. Monk had left the high school. We had lost a lot of seniors and things generally sort of deteriorated under Mr. Wallender. He actually just didn't actually have it as a band director, but I'm sure he was a good musician on his own part. During my high school career, we had 4 band directors, a different one each year. Of course, this was disappointing to me, but things were quite upset during those years because of World War II.

During the fall of 1940, I worked at a Department Store. First of all, I worked in the grocery department under Tony Lohr. I then started working in the clothing department, selling shoes and suits and so forth, mostly under two men named Ben and Harry. Working Saturdays in the grocery department was really quite a challenge. That fall was a difficult one as far as football was concerned because, as I stated before, I was a freshman probably playing 50% of the time as a right guard on the high school football team. Why was it bad? Well, I think we split the season, about 4 wins and 4 losses, and it was difficult because I was playing against juniors and seniors from other teams.

I can remember mainly one game that we played at Hurley, South Dakota, and I played against a couple of seniors. It was a rainy night and the field was muddy. I was eating mud most of the night and they found a weakness in our line on defense when I was there. I tried my best, but I was submarining most the night. That's where you fake up and go down and crawl along the ground trying just to block everything in the process. Well, let's just say I got murdered! It was a learning experience, but really tough. I had a good linebacker behind me, a junior named Cliff Bastemeyer. He was an excellent linebacker and good tackler, so he kept hitting me on the back of the butt and saying, "Get in there, Don!" I did my best. We lost that game down at Hurley, I think by 1 touchdown, but then there were better times ahead. As a football player, that was sort of a dismal season for me, but I was looking forward to when I would put on some weight and be able to pay some guys back. Our coach that year was Clair Ekeland.

In the fall of that year, I was in an operetta. I think it was called "The Student Prince." It was really peculiar, because when I look back on some of the pictures, I find myself standing by Mavis Heeren and I think we were coupled together as far as singing and so forth in the chorus, holding hands maybe; anyhow, she became my sister-in-law in years to come and she also was a neighbor of ours. The stars in that show were a boy named Ivan, and I forget the girl singer. I guess it was Marilyn Martini. They were the boy and girl who sang some solos from that particular operetta. Mrs. Arthur Nelson directed it. I also enjoyed the scholastic part of my freshman year, taking Freshman Algebra, Latin I, General Science, and American History. I think I did get all A's that year. I, of course, was playing in the band also. I was first chair with the French horn section and we had the usual fall and Christmas concerts.

There was an interesting experience in the fall of 1940, the famous snowstorm hit, and it went something like this. On a Saturday, it started to rain quite heavy and I used to always go over to the gym whenever I could and practice basketball. We had a good friend named Fred who had the keys because he would help clean around there, and so we would go in and shoot baskets and scrimmage and so forth on our own. I remember doing that in the afternoon on a Saturday and the rain turned to sleet in the evening.

Next, on Sunday (It was Nov. 11th, Armistice Day), my father and I, and several young people, were in the car driving up to Madison, South Dakota for a Luther League meeting. Dad had a new Pontiac, 1940, and we drove to Madison, which was 35 miles away. As time went on in the afternoon, the snow got heavier and heavier. It was called

"The Famous Blizzard of 1940." They also call it "The Armistice Day Storm." On the way back, we took some shortcuts to try to get home faster because the snow was already 15 in. deep, and in those days we had no snow tires. We got stalled out in the country, near Chester, South Dakota, and had to walk the fence line to a house and stayed overnight because of the severe storm. We were able to get home either the next day or the day after that, I can't remember for sure. The phone lines were down, so the family members were really worried about us, but we did make it home.

There were many people who were killed during that storm. According to records and the paper, I think there were approximately 40 duck hunters in Minnesota killed that weekend. They got caught up north in different sloughs and so forth and, of course, they waited until the last minute and couldn't get out, and so they froze to death. My brother-in-law, Dr. John Hermanson, stated that he went to Minneapolis for a football game at the University of Minnesota and he had to stay there for a couple of days.

Now we approach the basketball season. I was a freshman, playing on the "B" team and we had a great team. I believe we went undefeated. The "B" team consisted of me playing center, Don Bach and Jack Lauer as forwards, and Bill Briley and Dale Dunn at guard. We may have lost just 1 game. We always played before the varsity game. I also played a little with the varsity if they got way ahead. I thought for sure I was going to make the tournament squad because everything was going better all the time. I was scoring well. Also, we had a basket on the garage, and I would shovel snow off and play basketball outside almost every night, almost, when I would get home. We had lights put on the garage, too.

Then came the District Tournament and I was really disappointed because at the last minute, they picked a senior who had never played much instead of a freshmen (that was me) for the 10th guy on the tournament squad. But, then on the other hand, they didn't go very far that year. I think they won 1 game and then lost in the semifinals, so they were out of the tournament. In those days, it was a 2-day tournament. You played 1 game on Friday afternoon or evening, and Saturday you played in the afternoon and evening both. This caused a lot of strain on players; they would get pretty tired if they had a tough game.

As a freshman in track, I ran the mile. I always remember a couple of guys running the mile with me, especially Ivan Holmoe, who was a senior. At the end of the race, he even coughed up blood and that was really impressive to me. At that time, we were in the same district as the Flandreau Indian team. The Flandreau Indians could run like crazy and I was usually looking at the back of their trunks. My best time at that time was about a 5 min. 5 sec. mile, and I never really placed too high, but it taught me a lot about endurance and so forth. We did go to several track meets, but the highest I ever placed was 4th.

Then came the spring and we had music contests. Our band, I think at that time, was down somewhat and got a 2nd. Our band director really wasn't anything to call home about. He was not asked to come back, which was a blessing. His name was Mr. Wallender. Our chorus, however, under the direction of Mrs. Arthur Nelson, did great. We won a superior and were able to sing at the Grand Concert in Madison at the District Contest. I did enter a solo on the French horn, but they gave only 1 superior those years in the District, and I got runner-up or excellent instead of superior. I played the Nocturne from Midsummer Night's Dream and my accompanist was Mary Margaret Hermanson. I can remember playing that at Garden Club and different places. I would do solos at church, East Nidaros, West Nidaros, Willow Creek Lutheran Church, and Dell Rapids Lutheran Church.

In 1941, my grandfather became more ill during the early spring months and was bedridden, and about the middle of April 1941, he died. I felt real bad because I didn't get the chance to talk to him on that day. He was quite lucid until the end, according to my mother. They said he had a stroke. The doctor came to the house and pronounced him dead, and he was taken to the funeral home. In those days, funeral homes weren't really equipped to have the bodies lie in state in the funeral home, especially in small towns. So he was laying there in the living room of our house for 2 days after being embalmed. People would come and go and pay their respects. Mother had me go over and pat the side of his face and feel his hands, and certainly it did help me overcome my fear of death. Of course, feeling those places on his body showed me that they were almost as hard as stone, and cold. He and I had been very close the first 14 years of my life.

The day of the funeral was a very sad day. The funeral was held at our church and Dad did the funeral service. Since Peter Stensland (my grandfather) was brought up and had a farm in Colton, South Dakota (12 miles away), he was buried in the cemetery there. I rode in the hearse with my future father-in-law, Mr. John Hermanson, who was the undertaker at that time. I remember the day well because it was a cool, rainy day, and the roads were really quite muddy. After Grandfather died, we fixed up the bedroom so that the girls could stay there instead of staying on the studio couch downstairs when they came home from college.

In the summer of 1941, I ventured out and I got a job working for Graham Good Year Co. in Sioux Falls, working for Mr. Tuttle, who was a friend of my sister, Maureen. I worked real hard. I stayed at a place over in Sioux Falls, on Minnesota Avenue. I learned a lot about cars. I would run the gas pumps and wash cars. One day, I remember, I washed and waxed 15 cars and all, hand waxed! No machinery. And my arms, legs, and hands were just aching at the end of the day. I was 14, going on 15, so I could drive. You didn't have to have a driver's license. I was impressed by some of the rich people who would come and drive their Cadillacs down, and I would have to wash and wax their Cadillacs and drive them back to their owners. Then they would bring me back down to the station. How they ever trusted me with their cars, I can't believe it. Then I did oil changes and grease jobs and graduated up to tire repairs, and it was quite dangerous at times because the rims could explode on you, and so forth. I just really learned a lot about gas station work. My salary was $67.00 a month.

I had a room at a boarding house and that cost $6.00 a week. I would always bring back the excess to my father to keep an account for me. He had a little black book and I've got that somewhere, where he would also keep money for Paul and Olin. On weekends, I would hitchhike home because I didn't have a car. That was quite easily acceptable. People would pick you up. Sometimes I would have to walk all the way to the top of the penitentiary corner in SF and hitchhike from there. It was quite a walk. It was only 20 miles up Highway 77 to Dell Rapids. Sometimes I would have to take 2 rides to get there. Usually Sunday night, or early Monday morning, somebody would bring me down to work again.

Also, during the summer, I took a couple of weeks off to go to Colorado with my parents and my sister, Eunice. We drove out and Dad was dean at a Bible Camp at Fowler, Colorado. I was dreaming of great things in Colorado, but when I got to Fowler, I found out that it was on the eastern $1/3^{rd}$ of Colorado, literally a desert. We stayed at a ranch run by the Tjerholms, a very nice family. Later I met several of them at Augustana. We stayed at their home, which was on a ranch and it was quite impressive. It had irrigation ditches and we swam in them. The water was very muddy, but they said it was bacteria-free. I suppose with all that mud, it couldn't have been anything else. The current was so swift; it was really sort of fun. The water was only about 4 feet deep and it was really fast and furious. In other words, it was an irrigated farm. They had a lot of livestock there, too. As a sideline on this particular trip, we went to a place called Longmont, Colorado, and stayed there a couple of nights with a pastor and his family who were good friends of my dad.

Then we drove to Colorado Springs, went to the Garden of the Gods and Seven Falls, and then climbed Pike's Peak with the car up to 14,200 ft. This was very impressive to a 14 year-old boy that had not done much traveling in his life. My sister and I got along very well and took pictures, but in those days, they were little 2 x 3 and ½ size black & whites and really weren't very good. Also, I had my first dog, called Wimpy, and it was a fox terrier with black and white spotted ears and mostly white. I remember they cut off his tail and I was really upset about that. But, I was able to keep Wimpy for about a year, and then he died for some reason. He got run over or something.

This brings us to the fall of 1941. During the spring and summer, we heard all kinds of news reports from over in Europe that Germany had invaded Russia, and there were daily reports of the war from all over the globe in the papers. Japan had invaded China and Burma and Malaysia. During the fall months, we would hear news reports out of Washington that we were having some difficulty with Japan in the form of trade, embargos, and so forth. They would have their ambassador at the White House and so forth, talking with Roosevelt. They had sunk a gunboat in China, which was our gunboat, and we were really upset with them about this. By then, we were helping England as far as getting supplies to them and to Russia on a so-called lend/lease program. At the time, the Senate and the House were very anti-war, even though we knew eventually we were going to have to help out with England, but we felt safe in knowing that we were still a long way from war. Roosevelt, however, really felt that we should help these countries.

It hit home when our National Guard in Dell Rapids, Sioux Falls, and Flandreau was called up, and they were sent to Australia to start training for possible war in that area. A friend of mine, Elwood Peterson, was in that group. He was older then I was, of course, but I remember Elwood was one of those that were caught in the Philippines after the war started. He was in the Death March and Baton but he survived as a prisoner of war of Japan after 4 years.

Regarding my activities, I was a member of the football team again and we had a real good team. Again, I was playing right guard, but this time we had a new coach, Coach Simantel, who I liked real well. I was a regular by now, and I think we won 6 out of 8 games and were champions of the Sioux Valley Conference. We returned the favor to Hurley, South Dakota, by beating them in Dell Rapids. We also beat Parker and Centerville, and also we beat Garretson. As far as girls were concerned, I did date some. I had some dates with a Mary Forsch. I was really too busy to have girl-friends, but we got along real good; had a good time together. Even at that age, I was still real naïve (hard to believe!). I remember the first date we had after a show. We walked home and were starting to walk up the steps on a porch. It was snowing out, but nice weather. We talked a while and then she finally said, "Aren't you going to kiss me good-night?" Well, believe it or not, that was the first time any girl had ever asked me for that! Well, I obliged her and we got along real good. That's as far as it went.

After a few more dates, I started going with another girl. Her initials were M.S. and we went fairly steady for 3 or 4 months. She had been going with some older boys and really knew her way around, so that scared the hell out of me. That's when we broke that off. At that age, I was very idealistic, in confirmation and so forth. I still had my eyes set on probably being a minister some day, and I got teased quite a bit by other boys because I was a goody-goody boy, interested in athletics, music, and good grades in high school. In fact, I was teased about studying a lot and getting good grades. They teased me a lot, and of course all my life they teased me about being a P.K., or Preacher's kid.

Homecoming that year was a big event. I was the sophomore representative and Patty Peterson, at the last minute, was elected from the senior class to be queen, and her attendants were Edith Lyng, Mavis Heeren (my future sister-in-law), and Alice Elliot. I got to be good friends with both Ardyce and Mavis Heeren, our neighbor girls. Ardyce was 1 year behind me and Mavis was 2 years ahead of me. I hung around more with the athletic boys (Dale Dunn, Don Bach and Morgan Christensen) as time went on.

By now, I was first chair in the band, and we had an excellent band director named Willard Fjefar. He was an excellent trumpet player. The ironic thing was that he was in high school at Yankton High School when my sister Maureen was there and we knew him well because he had been in District music contests there and we would hear him play, and he was a brilliant player. Willard helped spur me on to great heights with the French horn. I also sang in the chorus under Mrs. Nelson, and she wanted me to sing solos all the time.

My sophomore year in high school was a banner year, mainly because it was just before we got involved in the war. World War II really was disruptive to high school and college careers. We started basketball practice, and since Ivan Holmoe had graduated from high school, I became the starting center at 6 feet 2 inches. At that time, I weighed about 170 lbs., sort of, as they said "A handsome brute." It was hard to believe, looking back, on how many things I was involved in. I was in a French horn quartet, a woodwind quintet, a male vocal quartet, chorus, band, and solos in both vocal and instrumental. So, later on, when it came to the District contest, I didn't know where I was going to be. I was involved in 6 superiors, if you can believe that.

In the fall of that year, we had a Brotherhood Father-Son Banquet and I was to play my French horn solo, and lo and behold, a senator was our speaker! He was a famous senator from South Dakota. After I got through playing, he gave a speech and he complimented me very highly. Also, we always had a Christmas pageant at the church, and I sang as one of the 3 Wise Men together with my oldest 2 brothers. At our house, mother would play the piano and we would all sing a lot together and do solos, and so forth.

Back to basketball. At that time, it was my favorite sport. We went through the season of 24 games, I think, and lost 1. When we went to the Coliseum to play Sioux Falls Washington, the day before the game, there was a newspaper clipping, which I still have. It showed me, Fred Lauer, and one of the stars from Washington High, advertising that "3 stars will appear tonight in the ball game." They named us and it was a nice clipping in the Argus. I had to start getting used to this because there were many favorable articles in the paper.

An interesting article before we played Hurley; after we beat them in double-overtime in their small gym (they had an undefeated team up to this point), there was a big splash in the Argus-Leader about the two stars, Fred Lauer and Don Odland from Dell Rapids, being 2 of the best high school players seen in that area for a long time. An interesting fact in Hurley was that my cousin Margaret, who became Margaret Reiners, was sitting under the basket. When I would shoot free throws, she would be yelling against me. I did meet her after the game with her folks, my Uncle Lawrence and Agnes Odland. That year, Coach

Simantel coached us. He was the only real good basketball coach I had in high school and he spent a lot of time with me, developing a hook shot and teaching me a lot of things. He would spend a lot of time after practice helping me with different moves and so forth.

Then came December 7th, 1941. It was a Sunday afternoon and I was at Mrs. Arthur Nelson's home for Luther League. We had a late afternoon meeting and lunch, and somebody ran into the house and said, "Pearl Harbor has been bombed!" We were all stunned, but we really didn't know what it would mean to all of our lives. I was just 15 years old. But in the next 3 or 4 years of high school and college, it would mean a very different kind of life for us all. We got ourselves next to the radio and turned it on. They were already meeting with Congress in Washington, and the next morning, December 8th, President Roosevelt declared war on Japan and declared war on Germany. I believe the declaration of war against Germany was 2 days later.

We had boys in the service because the tension had been rising in the fall of 1941 and some of the guys were volunteering already. I have in mind one of my friends who played football with me, and his name was James Cobb. Jim had joined the Navy and he was aboard ship, and he was a fireman. That means he was down below, helping stoke the fires. At that time, the ships were run on oil or coal. His ship was sunk by the Japanese shortly after Pearl Harbor and he died at sea. They had a funeral service for him in Dell Rapids, but he never returned home. He had just graduated in 1940.

The next few days after Pearl Harbor, we heard all the bad reports coming back in the form of pictures of Pearl Harbor, and the fact that close to 2,000 men, Navy, Army, and Air Force, had been killed. But in spite of all of this, we just continued to live as normally as we could. Very shortly after that, different things came out in the form of orders from Washington, rationing of meat, rationing of food, but mostly meat. You had to get food stamps for meat and so forth. Then gas rationing came. You had to get gas stamps. If you were in a doctor's family, minister's family, veterinarian's family or something like that, you were allowed more stamps then usual, but it certainly cut down on everything. It didn't actually go into effect for probably 6 months after Pearl Harbor.

In the spring of 1942, I was playing basketball and playing in the band, going to music concerts, etc. As far as the girls, I was dating Myrna Heeren, a cousin of Mavis. At that time, especially with gas stamps and so forth and rationing, high school kids were pretty much grounded. Anyhow, after a very successful basketball season, we entered the District Tournament. We won all 3 games of the Districts. Our leading scorer was Fred Lauer. I played center, Fred and Jack Lauer, and Tom Merry played forward. He was going with Mary Hermanson. Sonny Richardson and Phil Anderson were playing guard.

We became District champions of District 12, and we went to the Regional Tournament the following week at Brookings, South Dakota. We played a town called Oldham in the first game in the afternoon on a Saturday, and we beat them quite badly. Then we had to come back and play in the evening against a town called Hazel. We saw Hazel play in the afternoon and we were scared to death because they had a guy who would shoot a hook shot that was a mile long (not really), but he would go down the sidelines and he would hook it up. He would do this way out by the end line on the side and hook it so he wouldn't be guarded at all, and SWISH! He scored something like 28 points against us. He had scored 40 in the afternoon. But we held him to 28, and we beat them, barely.

So, here we were District and Region Champs, and we were going to the State Tournament! The State Tournament in 1942 was held in the Corn Palace in Mitchell, South Dakota. As usual, at State Tournament time, it snowed. We had a lot of spectators come from Dell Rapids. We didn't have school buses because it was a public school and it wasn't consolidated, so everybody had to be transported by car. We played the first game on a Friday afternoon against Alexandria, South Dakota. We lost a very close game by 4 points. We felt very badly because we felt we didn't play very good. We went on to play the next morning against Ogalala Indian Reservation, now called Rosebud. Of course, they were all Indians.

Nowadays, if you look at some of our tactics, you would think we were racist, but the only way we could beat them, it seemed like, was razz them a little. You never did it very loud vocally, but I remember one thing, even the coach told us to do this…He said, "Just go up to them as they are going to shoot and say 'Ugh, Ugh,'" and they would miss their shot. When I look back, it was sort of sad to do that to these guys. Fred Lauer got hot and I think he scored about 25 points. I got my usual 10, and those guys would say crazy things to us, too, so I guess it went both ways. They would say things like, "Put some snow on the ball." I don't know what that meant, but they kept on saying that all the time.

I think we beat them by about 4 points, a very different game. That was Consolation Semifinals, in the morning on Saturday. All day it was snowing and got real slushy, and we didn't know if our spectators would get back for the evening. We were now in the Consolation Finals. We played Britton, South Dakota, and won by 1 point. I think I scored 12 points, Jack Lauer scored about 12, and his brother, Fred, scored about 18 or 20. Well, we weren't cocky at that time, but we felt pretty good about the whole thing. We returned home champions of the consolation round, at least. We had quite a few seniors on the squad. Fred would graduate, and so would Sonny Richardson and Phil Anderson.

Then came my biggest episode thus far with the music contest. As I said before, I was in several events. I had really gotten pretty good with the French horn by now. I played "Horn Concerto" by Mozart. My accompanist was Mrs. Simantel, the coach's wife, and she had to transpose a lot so I could play a large share of my notes in open tones, which was very difficult, but this made it faster. I went to the District contest in Madison and won a superior. I played in the Grand Concert in the evening. I also sang in the Grand Concert that evening because I won a superior in vocal. By the way, Mary Margaret Hermanson won 1st in the clarinet.

Then they had what they called National Regional Contests. This was composed of maybe the Midwest region, but you were still National Champions if you won. Mary Margaret went along and she played her clarinet and she won 2nd in the National Regional and I played my French horn solo and was very complimented by the judge, who thought I should go on in music. I was only a sophomore in high school. I won 1st place in the National Regional in French horn solo, and I won 2nd place in the bass solo. So, by now I was becoming very proud of the collection of medals that I was getting.

At the end of that spring, a lot of my good friends who had been seniors in basketball and football while I was a sophomore had graduated. So, it was sad to see them leave because most of them volunteered for the Navy, Marine Corp, Air Force, and so forth. About that time, they opened up the Air base in Sioux Falls, SD, which had at its peak time, 45,000 soldiers there. Right after school was out I took my Lifesaving Course (Junior and Senior). The previous year, I had taken my Junior Lifesaving Course. Now I finished my Senior Lifesaving Course and I was hired as a lifeguard at the Dell Rapids beach. I was a lifeguard all summer, every day of the week. I think I was paid $100.00 a month for this job. I had quite a bit of authority, had 2 other guards under me, and had to watch the office, too, although it was run by an older girl.

By now we were having an influx of Air Force soldiers from Sioux Falls coming up to our beach. They would come up and have beer parties in the park, and this was almost uncontrollable. Then they would come over to the bath house and some of them would throw-up all over, and we'd have to get somebody to clean it up, usually me. We tried to discipline these guys and kick them out if they were too far-gone. Then they would go swimming. I don't know how many guys I pulled out of the water half-drunk and saved their lives, actually, because they were drowning. They just weren't used to swimming in a river.

Earlier in my life, I had won some swimming contests from pier to pier, so I was considered a pretty good swimmer. This was quite a challenge though, when you try to rescue somebody who is drunk and twice your size. Sometimes, I had to practically coldcock them and grab them by the hair to pull them in. In fact, sometimes you wondered if your life was in danger. We had several companies from Sioux Falls who would march all the way to Dell Rapids, 20 miles, on the road and then give marching parades down Main Street. I especially remember one time on a Saturday that the Negro Company came up. At that time, it was still segregated in the Army. The big thing that happened in our high school was that half of our faculty left, all the good ones, because the government offered them higher salaries to come down and teach radio and different classes at the Air Force Base, because that's mostly what the Air Force Base was about. I was teaching about radar and radio. So, as a result, Mr. Simantel left, Mrs. Arthur Nelson (who was Principal) left, and the coach's wife Gladys (who was our music teacher) left as well. In fact, it just enucleated our faculty.

CHAPTER 4

THE COURTSHIP BEGINS

If I speak in the tongues of mortals and of angels, but do
not have love, I am a noisy gong or a clanging cymbal. And
if I have prophetic powers, and understand all mysteries
and all knowledge, and if I have all faith, so as to remove
mountains, but do not have love, I am nothing. If I give
away all my possessions, and if I hand over my body so
that I may boast, but do not have love, I gain nothing. Love
is patient; love is kind; love is not envious or boastful or
arrogant or rude. It does not insist on its own way; it is not
irritable or resentful; it does not rejoice in wrongdoing, but
rejoices in the truth. It bears all things, believes all things,
hopes all things, endures all things.

(1 Corinthians 13:1-7)

In the spring of 1942, I had been double-dating with another couple. I was going with Marge Sagness, and Tom Merry (one of my friends from basketball and football) was going with Mary Margaret Hermanson, and we would double date together. This was supposed to be after the July 4th band concert in the park. She stated, "I think I'm going to have a date with Tommy, but if he doesn't show up, I'll go out with you." Well, we had the band concert. I was in a quartet that sang several barber shop things. We dressed up as a Barber Shop Quartet and played our concert at the amphitheater in the park. There was a big crowd there. Afterward, I put my instrument away and I sort of hesitated at the side of the amphitheater, and here comes Tom, and that was the end of that.

Well, I was persistent. The next day was on a Sunday. I called up Mary Margaret and asked her for another date and she said, "I'm free tonight," so we went to the Sunday night show together. We went back to her house afterwards. Right from the first, we seemed to hit it off real good. Well, this really presented a dilemma for her because she was the steady girl for Tom. In fact, they had grown up together. Their parents were very close, the families were close and it just seemed preordained that they were going to always be together. I think for quite a while Tom was quite bitter about the whole thing, although he never actually let on to me because we played basketball the next year together. So, that's the way it all began. We had many dates in the summer. Occasionally, he would butt back in and get a date, but that became less and less. In fact, in the fall of 1942, he started going with Marge Sagness and they were very steady as we were.

In the summer of 1942 Mary and I had just started dating. I was still lifeguard during the summer of 1942, besieged by large numbers of male Army/Air Force boys coming up to the beach to swim and have parties in the park. I don't know how many I rescued from the river, but at least 10 or 12. That part of my job wasn't very good, except I was glad to do something for them. Other than that, I did swim. I got a good tan all summer and took good care of the beach. I had a couple of assistant lifeguards with me. I took it real serious. I would sit up there hour after hour watching the beach. A lot of the evenings would be spent with my newfound friend, Mary Margaret Hermanson, but interspersed with that were a few dates that she still had with her old, steady boyfriend, but they were becoming fewer. I just remained in the background a little more and became more patient for a while until school started in September 1942.

In the fall of 1942, my brother Olin was in his last year at Augustana and on the football team that went undefeated. Augustana was a member of the North Central Conference for the first year, under their coach, Leftie Olson. I saw all of their home games. It was very exciting because they were able to beat the University of South Dakota, University of North Dakota, University of Omaha, University of Northern Iowa, and Morningside, and went undefeated in the conference and won the title! Also during that fall, my brother Olin would bring football players back from Augustana to eat at our house (Ray Griffith, Don Halverson, Ed Byre, and Ray Sandvig). That was exciting on its own merit.

As far as high school was concerned, it was a problem. We had a new band director. We had a new coach. We had a new vocal music instructor. Our band director was Ralph Smith and he came with good recommendations, but it was a disaster. He would take us out marching and he was a great one to talk to people along the way, and sometimes I didn't think he was too bright. The band would trick him. While he was talking to somebody along the way, we would double-time and triple-time march, get around the corner, and then be quiet for a while. We would keep on walking and would lose him, and he wouldn't know where the band was.

Then I had him for some physics and chemistry and lots of pranks were pulled on him there as well. Some of the kids (and not me, because I was still a serious student) would crawl under the chemistry tables and attach test tube holders onto his pants and his coat, and then later on he would discover this and get mad. He would start to stutter and he wouldn't know what to do. I did okay grade-wise, but it was very frustrating because a lot of us students felt we knew as much or more than he at that time. He was also our band instructor, as I stated before.

Our coach was by the last name of Gilliland. He also taught math in school and I did real well under him in math. I got along good with him both in football and basketball, except for the first week of practice. Well, we would usually start off earlier in practice, around the last week in August after I got done being lifeguard. We called him "Coach Gilly." It was during the second week of football practice and apparently Gilly noticed when I was blocking and tackling a dummy out in practice that just before the impact of blocking, I would shut my eyes. I was a bad habit, but I did it. So, he kept egging me on to block harder, and at that time I was about 6 feet 1 inch and 170 lbs., fairly good sized. I suppose they could say I was "lean and mean" (Ha Ha!). At the last minute, after egging me on and getting me to block harder all the time on the dummy, he pulled away. I went flying through the air and landed on my right shoulder. I had injured my right shoulder before the first game of the season was played!

I went to the doctor and he said I had a separated sternoclavicular joint on the right side. Now, I know that's a serious injury, but at the time, I would do anything to play in the games. My mother and my older brothers thought I should take the season off, but my dad was emphatic that I would be playing football. He talked to the coach and to the doctor, who was Dr. A.F. Grove, and they agreed that I could miss the first game. After that, they strapped my shoulder down real hard and put me in a brace to wear, and then put shoulder pads on top of that. I played the rest of the season, which, in retrospect, was a mistake. Our season wasn't too good as we had lost a lot of seniors from the year before, and the senior class now ahead of us was not really talent-laden with football players. Although, they did have good basketball players in that class.

I believe we lost to Flandreau, 0-12. I think we won most of the rest of our games, but it was becoming apparent that the war effort was really cutting into our style of high school activities. It was getting harder and harder to get enough gas to go very far to games. Scheduling became a problem because of this. Because of the lack of teams to play, and the fact that other teams were experiencing the same problem, we even reverted from the 11-man game that we usually played, to an 8-man game. I remember we went up to Elkton, South Dakota, and we soundly beat them. At that time, it continued to be the fathers of the team members (including my father) who were in charge of hauling team members to games. Very few spectators could go because of the shortage of gas.

During the fall of 1942, one of my former music comrades who played a baritone in the band was killed at an Air

Force base, when a plane crashed. They brought his body back to Dell Rapids for a funeral service and burial, and these were hard times. We were taking more casualties in the war and some of my brother's fellow classmates in college were killed also. We learned that one of the former high school members was captured by the Japanese and was in a prison camp. Most of the boys I played basketball with in the spring of 1942 had already joined the Navy, Air Force, and Army, and a lot of them were already being sent overseas.

Our vocal music teacher was good. It was Gwendolyn Williams. She was not only a good chorus director, but she was also a good instructor and a good singer herself. I don't want to give the opinion that we didn't have fun in school. We did, in spite of a lot of the tragic things happening in the world around us. Fortunately, at the time, we didn't have TV to show the casualties overseas, and a lot of things were watered down by propaganda so that we didn't really know how bad it was. But, I'll say one thing; the whole country was behind the war effort.

Mary and I were going pretty steady by October and double-dating with either Jack Lauer and his fiancée, Dorothy Wicks, or Tom Merry and Marge Sagnes. We would go to shows together and there were school parties, too. And, of course, there was the Dell Rapids Pavilion. There were weekly dances there, and believe it or not, I learned to dance at that particular time. In fact, jitterbugging was real popular, and I had one of the girls in my class teach me how to jitterbug one night. I was busy also with church choir. I faced up to my dad once and asked him if he cared if I went dancing and he stated that I could go dancing, but not with his permission. I was his way of saying, "You can go, but I'll look the other way."

Also, I liked to play pool a lot, and the only place to play pool in town, or billiards, was at the local pool hall. I would sneak in the back door and play 9-ball, 8-ball, and rotation, and really got pretty good at it. Pretty soon, the older guys in the pool hall wanted to bet with me and we would play for a quarter a game. That part, I never told Dad (that I played for money), but I told him it was the only place in town that I could play pool and I loved to play it, and it was a good sport. So he treated that the same as the dancing problem. He didn't really argue with me about it. He was a very fine father. You always had that feeling that both he and my mother loved you, and you dearly loved them, but there was no such thing as kissing and hugging, except with mother and son, but not dad and son. That is, until my oldest brother left for the Navy. I'll cover that later.

I gradually recovered from the injury to the right shoulder through the fall and the end of football season came. We had a winning season, although we won just a few more than we lost. Then came our forte, and that's basketball. We had just come off a wonderful year at the end of the basketball season in early 1942, and we approached the '42-'43 basketball season with high hopes, even though we lost our best scorer, Fred Lauer, and our best guard, Phil Anderson. We also lost Sonny Richardson, another guard. Since I was a starter the year before, I was right in the thick of it. I grew a little by then. I was 6 foot 2 inches, and weighed about 175 lbs. At that time, I was considered fairly tall for a center, except we did have a center in the district who was 6 foot 6 inches, and that caused a problem.

We had a very successful basketball season. We won both the Big-8 Conference and the Sioux Valley Conference. I think at the end of the season we were 19-1, losing one game to Madison Central, which was considered an A-Class school and we were B-Class. We had a Christmas tournament, and we won that. Before the mid-year (before the middle of January), when the first semester ended, Jack Lauer, Bill Briley, and Carter Mower played with us, but they were mid-year students so their eligibility was over as of the semester. That left us with the following players: Jerome Anderson and Dale Dunn as guards, I played center, and Donald Bach and Tom Merry played forwards.

We went on to the District Tournament in mid-February and we won our games over Chester, Flandreau, and Trent. We became District 12 Champions. Then we went on the Region 3 Tournament in Brookings. This was 4 teams in the Region, like it is in Minnesota. Again, the same rules applied as the year before where you had to play in the Region in the afternoon and evening both of Saturday. This also was done to save mileage on cars because people were allowed to go to these games, but they had to save up their gas stamps. We played Oldham in the semifinals in the afternoon and beat them quite handily.

In the evening, we played in the finals against Volga, which now is called Sioux Valley (a team near Brookings). This was one of the toughest games we had ever been in. They were tall, very good players. In those days, the scores of the games weren't as big as nowadays. We played tougher defense. They allowed you to get a little more aggressive on defense. We were behind about 6 points at the half. Near the end, it looked like disaster for our cause. In a fairly low-scoring game, we were behind 23-31, with ½ minute to go. We put on the press, and miracles do happen. We were able to intercept a couple of passes and make a couple of quick baskets. Their team panicked somewhat, and in that last minute and ½, we didn't let them stall, and we hardly ever let them get out of their backcourt. We scored 9 points in 1 and ½ minutes and won the ballgame, 32-31!

The crowd just went bananas! In fact, one of the young fellows in our class, who was an excitable fan, came running out of the stands and hit one of our players (Don Bach) on the head and cut his head open! But, that got stitched up and fixed. Would you believe it? We were going to the State Tournament 2 years in a row! We actually felt so sorry for that other team after beating them that way (because they were really a fine bunch of fellows) that we got together and signed a card to them as being good sports. They had had complete control of the game and a bunch of rinky-dinks came out and beat them.

Well, we got the job done. We then moved on to Aberdeen, South Dakota, for the State High School B-Tournament, which was a big thing. The bad part of it was that it was 200 miles from Dell Rapids. Nowadays you see busloads and literally hundreds of people following a team, but it was not the case then. There was no television, of course, and the games were broadcast statewide, so that my brothers stated later on that they sat in the chemistry lab at Augustana and listened to the games, unable to get there because of the gas shortage. My dad was able to come up with Dr. Dunn, who was the father of one of the team members. Dr. Dunn, being a veterinarian, could get extra gas stamps, so he took some of the fathers with him. Another carload of cheerleaders came along and a third car came along with a bunch of the girlfriends of the team members. That's the way that went. I don't think we had 25 people there from Dell Rapids.

Here again, we had to play 3 games in 2 days, which was going to be a problem for us. In the first game, we played the Rosebud Indians (which used to be the Ogalala team from the Rosebud Reservation). Here again, the scores were lower in those days, but it was a very tight game and we won, 26-24! In the second game (we played on Saturday afternoon, and the first game was played on Friday after-noon) we met DeSmet, South Dakota. DeSmet had won 26 games in a row and was loaded with talent. We probably played the best game in my entire high school career, and especially I played my best game. We were ahead at the 1st quarter, 2nd quarter, and 3rd quarter, and won the ballgame! But, to this day, I never could find a recording of it on the radio. It would have been nice to have because it was just a tremendous game. We won, 51-41! I was able to score 22 points. In fact, everything I threw up there went in. We were really bushed. The other team that played in the afternoon had an easier.

Mobridge was next. They played the first game in the afternoon while we played the second game in the afternoon. So, that meant we didn't get through with our game until about 5:00. Coach had us go have a light lunch and lay down and rest. But everybody was so keyed-up it was difficult to relax. We had to come back at 7:30 and dress for the final game against Mobridge, South Dakota, and I believe it started around 8:30. By then, of course, we were meeting the top-notch teams. They had a center that was 6 feet 5 inches, and I was only 6 feet 1 and ½ inches tall. Well, we gave it our best shot and we lost in the finals by 1 point. For a long time, I played that game over. In my dreams, I would sink the winning shot, but it was not to be. Being runner-up in the State Tournament and consolation winner of the State Tournament the year before were quite the honors. Further honors were coming my way, and I was picked for the All South Dakota Basketball Team.

As we all know, tournament time brings snowstorms. All of us basketball players were real excited, the ones especially who had girlfriends at the games. They had an All High School party after the game at Aberdeen with pop and hors d'oeuvres, and a dance, and we were having such a good time. But our time was short because the chaperones that brought the cheerleaders and the girls to the tournament had stated that we had to get going for home. What a disappointment! But, that's the way things would go sometimes. They wanted to get home before the snow got worse, so off they went. The rest of us stayed there overnight and went home the next day.

Well, at that time, I always figured being a senior the

next year; we would have a shot at the big prize. So, even though we were disappointed coming home as runners-up, we had a lot of publicity and felt that we had a good team. This was in the spring of 1943. My brother Paul was a junior at Augustana, and my brother Olin was a senior and would graduate from Augustana soon. My sister Maureen had a baby in November of 1942, so I was an uncle by now. We still lived in the house up on the hill. I was still playing the French horn in the band, but things weren't going too good with our band. It was quite disorganized, and this was a disappointment. But because of all the gas shortages and limited travel, the music contests that year were scratched. Mary and I were still going together, still going to shows and dances and school parties, Luther League, and so forth, together. She also sang in the choir at church.

One interesting thing happened Easter Sunday, as I remember. I was going to sing "The Holy City," which is a favorite of a lot of people and me for Easter Sunrise Service. I had never sung at the Sunrise Service on Easter, and of course, that's at 6:30 in the morning. Mary was accompanying me. I was standing in the choir loft and she was down below playing the piano. I got through 2/3rds of it and there was a place where I could comfortably quit and nobody would know the difference. I was having some trouble with a frog in my throat, which people didn't notice, but I certainly was having problems. So, without telling her I just sat down, and she wondered what happened to me, but she was able to bring the piece to an end. Just one of those little things, but it was embarrassing.

In the spring, I was in the play. I played some old railroad engineer, and I can't remember exactly what the play was about. I was in the junior play and Mary was in the senior play. She was a year ahead of me in school because she had skipped a year in grade school. She played the lead in the play. The title was something like "Here Comes

April" or something. And lo and behold, Tom Merry was her lead man. I said to myself, "Here we go again!" Well, we were still going steady, but when I went to the play, I couldn't believe it. I tried to calm my nerves a little, but near the end of the play, they went into a clinch that seemed to last forever with some kissing in it. I said to myself, "Oh, brother!" Well, I don't think I said too much to her about it, because I realized it was part of the play, but I always felt that he really took full advantage of the situation.

At the Junior-Senior banquet that year, Mary and I went together. Because of the shortage of red meat, a bunch of us juniors went out to get some meat and we did the best thing we could think of, we went pheasant hunting. There ware about 40 in our class and 28 in her class. With all the boyfriends and girlfriends, I suppose there were close to 60 at the banquet, in the basement of the Lutheran Church. A bunch of us juniors had to help get the meat together, so we went out and hunted for pheasants. That seemed to be a good solution, and it was. I think in just a couple of days, we rounded up 40 pheasants, cleaned them, and helped the people in the kitchen cut the meat off. We had creamed pheasant, plus other things (pumpkin pie and so forth) at the Junior-Senior banquet. Mary was President of the senior class and I was President of the junior class, so we each made our speeches and everything went real good. Of course, she looked beautiful as ever. I believe her formal was a light blue color. I think after the banquet, 2 or 3 of us couples went to a show at the Egyptian Theatre.

Then graduation came. I went over to Augustana to see my brother graduate. Also, Mary graduated from Dell Rapids High School with a lot of my good friends a year ahead of me, especially the ones I played with as teammates in basketball and football. A lot of these young fellows I wouldn't see for a long time because they entered the military service right after school was out. Several of them would be destined to be in the service for the next 2 and ½ - 3 years. My brother Olin went and enlisted into the officer's training program and he was sent to Notre Dame to become an ensign in the Navy. In the fall of 1943, he was sent overseas as the Captain of an LST boat. He was shipped to the South Pacific, but before he left, he came home. He looked so nice in the Navy uniform. I believe, up to that time, that's the only time I ever saw my father become quite emotional. When he hugged my brother, he cried. We all realized that this was a very serious time for him to be going overseas.

My summer of 1943 was spent working at John Morrell Co. Meatpacking Plant in Sioux Falls. I stayed in Sioux Falls for while and then after that. I hitchhiked back and forth, as I didn't have a car at that time, and I worked in the freezing department. Being a tall, lanky, young fellow, I certainly got some tough jobs. I would lift 100-120 lb. Boxes of meat all day long and stack them, sometimes 6 and 8 high. Sometimes we would stack these 60 lb. frozen meat boxes on carts until we had a big load, and then we would pull the 2-handed cart. We would transfer the meat on railroad cars and ship it all over the world for the servicemen and so forth. A lot of the packages would be labeled "London destination" or "European allies." I worked all summer, and met some real nice people at the packing plant. In fact, 50 years later, one of the men I worked with in the freezer department at Morrell's would be a patient of mine. His name was Peter Schwarz. On weekends, I would be off, of course, but a lot of times we would work on Saturday and be off just Sunday, and Mary and I would be able to go out on dates then.

In the summer of 1943, I believe, my sister Eunice and her boyfriend, who she met at the Air Base, Don Aucutt, were married. They were married on May 5, 1943. My father married them at the Lutheran Church. I played my French horn and Mary played the piano for me. I believe I played "Berceuse." My cousin, Evelyn Granskou, played the cello. After the wedding, there was a reception at our house. Late that evening, toward the end of the reception, Mary and I took Eunice and her new husband, Don, and drove them to Sioux Falls, to the train to take off. Of course, he was in the service and I believe they were going on their honeymoon to Tomah, Wisconsin, at the Air Base where he was stationed.

Then the fall of 1943 came. I was studying my senior year in high school. By then, we had moved from the house on the hill down to a new location. It was an older house, which was the Moe house, north of the Lutheran Church. This was very convenient. It was a 2-story house with quite big rooms. It made it handy because I became the janitor at the church. My dad would help me with mowing lawns and cleaning up the church every week. It also was easy to go to school. The school was only 1 and ½ blocks away. It was going to be different as a senior because Mary was gone. She was off to South Dakota University, as a freshman there.

By now, both of my sisters were married and my oldest brother was overseas in the Navy. Paul, my brother who was 4 years older than I, was a senior at Augustana and he was majoring in Pre-Med. I was starting to think about college also. Mary joined the Kappa Alpha Theta Sorority at the University of South Dakota and was majoring in Sociology. In the fall, I went down there 2 or 3 times and she came home 2 or 3 times, but the distance was starting to strain our relationship. I was trying also to concentrate on sports and music and my own senior year in high school. I was elected President of the student body. Our class was about 36 members now because some of the class members prematurely left to go into the service.

I had a very successful football season. We had a new coach, Noel Muller, my brother-in-law's brother. Noel also taught classes, and later became our basketball coach as well. So, within the space of 4 years of high school, I had a different coach every year and a different band instructor every year. We had a new band person who was Mrs. Bremer. She was an improvement over the last one that we had, but was certainly not as good as the first two we had (Beryl Monk and Willard Fjefar).

Our football team went undefeated. Because of the distance problems, we played Flandreau High School twice and the Flandreau Indians once. We won all 8 of our football games. I had been growing some and I was the same height, but about 180-185 lbs., and played end on defense and end on offense. By now, it was payback time. Because of my size, I was able to pretty much break up plays coming around the end, almost at will. I really had ambitions to play further on in college. I did have some dates that fall, different girls, but nobody steady. After all, you had to have some escorts to go to certain activities, but on the other hand, I was a loner a lot of times, too, going out with the guys. Up until this time, I really took training seriously, as far as no booze, and there was no such thing as drugs in high school. People knew about marijuana, but there was none available, and I didn't smoke at all, although some of the guys did smoke.

Then basketball season came, and we again had a very successful season. I believe during my sophomore, junior, and senior years we played between 66 and 68 games and lost only 3 regular season games and 3 tournament games. We became a heavily favored team my senior year almost every time we went to play basketball because we had almost the same team that had been runner-up in the State Tournament, except for one member, Tom Merry, who graduated. Replacing him was Chuck Berge.

We had dreams of winning the State Championship. We won both conferences again, and we upped our competition. We played Pipestone twice and beat them. We played Jasper twice and beat them badly. At that time, Jasper was pretty good. We beat Chester, which was our biggest threat, 3 times. We beat them 2 times during the regular season and one time during a Christmas Holiday Tournament. We lost one game during the season to Madison Central. They went on to the State "A" Class Tournament. That was only 4-5 points that we lost by. Coming into the District Tournament, we faced Flandreau first, and I had a red-hot game and scored 20-25 points, I'm not sure. During the Semi-Finals the next day we played Egan. Egan's claim to fame that year was that they had a boy who scored 55 points in one game and beat a team called White, South Dakota, 110-20. They were undefeated, and we knocked them off during the semifinals.

We did develop a problem in the Districts. On the morning of the tournament, the coach had an argument with a couple of our best players in the classroom and the next day, they skipped class. So, then he kicked them off the team, and I think if we would have had a vote, the rest of us would say, "Let them stay off the team," but he reneged on it and brought them back. Things didn't go too well. This caused a little friction, and during the final game against Chester, who we had beaten 3 times (2 times quite badly) during the year, they became very hot. They really would sink all their shots, and our dreams of a State Championship came to an end in the District Finals. We lost the District Finals by 3 points. I absolutely couldn't believe it! Boy, was this a downer. However, I didn't have long to think about it.

Because of the war problems and my age of 18 coming up pretty soon, I was trying to get in some college before I would become 18 so I could maybe get a break and become an officer or something like that. So, by previous arrangement with the principal and superintendent, and having good grades and so forth, I was able to leave high school in March of my senior year, just after the State Tournament was over, and went to South Dakota University for the 3rd quarter, which would be my 1st quarter of the freshman year for me.

When I went to register, they asked me what I was going to major in and what I was going into. I told them Chemistry or Biology, probably Chemistry. I said, "Well, my brother's already down here. I'll just sign up fro Pre-Med."

Of course, then Mary and I got back together on a dating schedule. She was busy with her sorority and I was busy studying, and the 1st quarter was over in late May. I had straight "A's" and I was able to go back to Dell Rapids to graduate with my class. This was sort of a peculiar way to graduate from high school. It's a funny thing nowadays that some of the kids are doing this again, that is, going to college in combination with their senior year in high school. I'm not so sure I agree with this because those years go by too fast anyhow. So, what did I do during the summer? I went to full-time summer school and boy was it hot down there in Vermillion, South Dakota! I was taking Chemistry and Math, and by September of 1944, I would be registered, starting as a sophomore at the University of South Dakota, picking up a whole year's credits within a quarter and full-time summer.

During the summer, one thing did happen that was funny. I was with Don Hillan and another boy, and we were so warm! We couldn't get into the swimming pool at the outdoor park so Don got the idea to go over to the college gym because there was a pool over there. We got over to the pool and it was a real hot evening, and it was all locked up, of course. This was probably 10:00 at night. He just took off his shoe and he banged the door window, broke it, and reached in and unlatched the door. We got into the field house and then proceeded to the pool and stashed our clothes next to the spectators little stadium they have and then went swimming in the nude, 3 of us guys. Lo and behold, here comes a searchlight. Some night watchmen came down the hallway and he saw we were splashing around in the water. He came in there and gave us hell. He got us out of the pool and made us get dressed, and he took us right down to the President of the University. Well, President I.D. Weeks said he would take care of things. After he left, President Weeks sort of winked at us and said, "Fellows, you had better pay for that window," which we did. The upshot of the whole thing was that Don stayed at his house. He had a room there and babysat with his kids, and he wasn't about to turn us over for breaking and entering or anything like that. He just laughed about it and said, "Did you have a good swim?" And he also said, "I was young once, too." So that part was over. It was hard that summer because I had to study a lot and I was staying upstairs in a little house. We would go down to the Varsity (that was the local hubbub), a café on the top floor, and the basement was where everybody went to dance and drink beer and so forth. I guess I'll have to honestly say I learned how to drink beer at South Dakota University. I also met a lot of good friends there.

During the summer months Mary Hermanson was in Dell Rapids and I was in Vermillion. Again, we were separated for a while, which probably was for the best, at least at that time. Although, we were still dating. During the spring term I took ROTC, so I got into the military a little, as far as drilling and so forth was concerned. Then came the fall months of 1944. I took German, Chemistry, Biology (Zoology), and Math. I would be 18 on October 23rd.

There was no football team. We played intramural football because on the campus of South Dakota University at that time were about 500 ASTP Army students. There were sorority dances and school events. One thing did happen. By now, Tom Merry was in the U.S. Navy. He came home on leave and I asked one of the sorority girls where Mary was and they said, "Oh, she went to Dell Rapids with Tom Merry." So, things were sort of strained for a while between Mary and me, and I started dating another girl or two down at the University. One went by the initials A.O., and she was in the Pi Phi Sorority. For a while, I was working in a kitchen serving meals to make a little dough on the side. I was just doing some substituting work for another guy.

During the fall of 1944, I stayed at the SAE House and I pledged to SAE but I didn't become an active member of the fraternity because I was going to be leaving. I was involved in ROTC. My brother, Paul, was now graduated from Augustana and was in the so-called V5 program of the Navy as a medical student, wearing his Navy uniform and going to medical school at South Dakota University. During November, I went out for basketball at South Dakota University. Our coach was Rube Hoy. He was a legendary coach at USD and boy did he work us out. We learned how to run the fast break and a lot of things I didn't learn in high school.

Looking back, the only real coach I had was Floyd Simantel, as a sophomore. The last 2 years, the coaches were not that good, as far as teaching anything, and we just did it on our own a lot of times. Now, I was under the tutelage of a master of the trade. I was playing forward, Tom Looby at center, Dick Lindquist and Art at guards, and Benny at the other forward. My basketball season was going to be very abbreviated, but we did have a chance to go to Minneapolis and on a Friday night we played Hamlin University. We got beat, but we had fun.

While I was up there, and that was my first big trip like that, we stayed at the Curtis Hotel, and Coach Hoy gave us some spending money. I went to a stage show and saw Artie Shaw, a famous band director. We also went across town on the streetcar to see a friend of one of the guys. Casper was his name, and he was a football player at the University of Minnesota, whom we had known at Aberdeen, South Dakota in high school. I had dreams at that time of playing football there, but these never worked out. On Saturday night, we played the University of Minnesota in basketball, in the Williams Arena. They had a very tall team. We didn't have too much height, but we kept with them in the 1st half. We lost by 12 points in the 2nd half. We came back to the University of South Dakota the next day on Sunday. We had a real good time and it was a very memorable experience. We played about 3 more games before Christmas vacation. I had finished the first quarter of my sophomore year, and I was draft eligible and draft registered. In early December, I received a "Dear Donald, Greetings from your President" letter. "You are notified as of now that you will be drafted on such & such a date." I went down to the Navy station and talked to them, and wanted to get into the radio or radar technician field, if I could (a special program).

CHAPTER 5

OFF TO THE NAVY

The Lord is my shepherd, I shall not want. He makes me lie down in green pastures; he leads me beside still waters; he restores my soul. He leads me in right paths for his name's sake. Even though I walk through the darkest valley, I fear no evil; for you are with me; your rod and your staff - they comfort me. You prepare a table before me in the presence of my enemies; you anoint my head with oil; my cup overflows. Surely goodness and mercy shall follow me all the days of my life, and I shall dwell in the house of the Lord my whole life long.

(Psalm 23:1-6)

———⇒●⇐———

O
n January 12th, I left from Minneapolis and was sworn in with a group of fellows from South Dakota into the U.S. Navy at Ft. Snelling. We took the train from Sioux Falls to Minneapolis, and then we took the train from Minneapolis to the Great Lakes Training Station north of Chicago, Illinois. We arrived there in the early morning hours of January 12th. We got off the train with our meager belongings and it was −12 degrees. We were met by some Navy officers, and they herded us like a bunch of cattle, marching us double file over to the Mess Hall for breakfast. We stood outside, freezing, thinking they would never open the door. They finally opened the door and we went inside and had breakfast, which was pretty good. Everything seemed to happen that day. We went to a real large room, and had to strip down to our shorts. We went through lines and got our uniforms, and then went through another line and got a quick physical. That was the briefest physical I had ever seen.

Very shortly, we went through another door and guys were fainting like flies. They were giving all kinds of shots in both sides. Some of the guys walked ahead of us and they still had the needles in their arms. That sure did a lot of good for your psychic. In the space of one 24-hour period, in addition to eating Navy chow, I got a Navy uniform and

Navy shots, and a mattress and a double bunk bed (upper and lower). I was on the upper bunk and my pal, John Norby, from Chicago, was on the lower bunk. I felt sorry for Johnny because he was rather short and heavy-set. He was very smart, but very tenderhearted, and I didn't know how he would ever get through basic training.

I had always been in athletics and did a lot of muscle training and running and so forth, so even though it wasn't a piece of cake for me, it was a real hardship for some of the guys. We had to run the obstacle course in cold weather and one thing I could never do was climb a rope, but I had to. We had to run as hard as we could and climb about a 20-foot wall, grab onto some ropes, and pull ourselves over. These were all timed. While I was at the Great Lakes, I also joined the Great Lakes Basketball Team. There were quite a few teams. I had played at USD, and there were 2 guys from Texas as well. It turned out to be a pretty good team. We won our league championship. The training was vigorous. I really felt top-notch physically.

I tried out for and sang in the Great Lakes Choir. There were 60 voices, all men, and pretty soon I was singing solos with the Great Lakes Choir on Sundays. We would broadcast every Sunday. It was sort of nerve-wracking at times because I would be singing before probably 1,500 fellows in church. We had a giant church that was actually the Quonset where we had basketball and everything, but they put chairs up on Sunday morning. Then they had some try-outs for a big night of entertainment. We got to meet the Great Lakes E Band. They had about 30 members in that band. These included former members of the Glen Miller Band and the Tommy Dorsey Band. These members had been drafted and put a band together. It was a great sound. In fact, they wanted me to transfer over to the music department of the Navy to be in the band and tour around the bases.

I didn't get very far in trying to get that job done. I did

try-out singing, however, with the band. So, here I was, standing before the microphone with spotlights and this big band behind me, singing a couple of love songs to this crowd of over 2,000 sailors. On the same program were stars from different parts of the service (the Navy). After getting through the singing, they hooted and howled. It made me feel good that I had tried out, at least. I was at Great Lakes for 6 weeks. Then I had a week's leave. I went home by train, and my folks met me. At that time, I was back together with Mary. We spent almost every evening together. As I was leaving to go back to the base by train, I'll never forget my aunt. It was Aunt Gilma. She was up at our house visiting because her husband had just died in New Guinea in the service. He was a chaplain. She put her arms around Mary as I walked out of the house to go with dad down to the train in Sioux Falls, and she said to Mary, "That's the way my Ole walked out of my life." That made Mary feel real good (Ha-Ha!).

Back to the Great Lakes. I passed my tests and I was able to go into the radio technician and radar division (RT program). I went to Herzyl Junior College in southwest Chicago. It was an old junior college that had been taken over by the Navy, and I spent a month there. This was in higher math and radar and technician problems. It was a short course in a lot of things, but very intensified. At the end of each week, we took tests. If you didn't pass, you just flunked out and you could repeat one week. If you didn't pass the second time, you would be shipped out to sea. Talk about having a gun to your head. Some of my best buddies were shipped right out to sea.

I finished the course in 4 weeks and then was sent back to the naval station at Great Lakes for 3 months of intensive work in radio and radio repair. During those 3 months, Mary was able to come down to Chicago once and she stayed with her Aunt and Uncle out at Evanston. While she was there, we went to a show and she said she would never forget the show because it was "30 Seconds Over Tokyo" with Van Johnson, and it was a tearjerker. It didn't make her feel very good. I saw her off on the train and she went back to Dell Rapids.

Also, while I was in Chicago, I met my brother Paul and his girlfriend, Barbara Ruhl. We tried to figure out how I could ride the train over there on a 72-hour pass. We had restrictions that we weren't supposed to leave within 40 miles of the base and this was over 100 miles. My brother Paul was in a Navy uniform and we got on the train and I really had no authority to do this, but we sat 3 abreast on the train and ran out to Barbara's hometown in Ohio. I was sleeping, but my brother would fake things for me with the SP's (that's Shore Patrol) as they would pass, and always say that I was with him. I was able to get to stay overnight for a couple of nights at the Ruhl house and met the family. I then went back to Chicago and had no problems getting back to the base this time.

While in Chicago, we would go on leave during weekends to shows and also to the USO for dancing and so forth. I met some nice young people in Chicago. We went to see Doris Day singing on stage at the Oriental Theatre. Then I was transferred to Corpus Christi, Texas. I decided to join the Navy Air Corp. We had a choice to go there or to California. I would be stationed at an Air Base, and I would be part of the Navy Air Corp. We took a long hot trip on the train to Texas. The commanding officer said we had to wear wool blues instead of whites, which was ridiculous, but a lot of things in the service were ridiculous. This was June.

I'll start out with my trip to Corpus Christi, Texas. We first transported to the Chicago Union Railroad, and did this by bus from Great Lakes, Illinois. We got all loaded up with our belongings and got on the train at Chicago. Our commanding officer insisted on us wearing Navy blues, wool of course. And to top it off, the train trip became hotter as we went south. I don't think I was ever so grimy and dirty as I was on that trip, because it was hot on the train and there was very poor ventilation. It was a Pullman. We had a day car, so it was crowded. We all wanted to put on our Navy whites, which were lighter cotton, but he insisted we dress up. This was ridiculous because we weren't very dressed up by the time we got there.

On the way, I noticed several things. We were able to go to the dining car and of course the train was just loaded with civilian people and service people. The meals were fair, but I noticed as we traveled back through the train that there were cars that were totally black and cars that were totally white. This was at the end of the war and the segregation in the troop levels was still apparent. The train was also loaded with Army veterans who were being transported across the country after being in Europe. After the Germans had surrendered, these troops were being transported across our country to San Francisco to embark on the long trip further west to help with the war in the Pacific. I talked to several of these veterans and they weren't happy by any means. They hadn't been allowed any leave and they had already been in Europe for 3 years and now they were being transported west.

After a 48-hour trip, we arrived in Corpus Christi, Texas. We were then transported by bus to the naval air station at Ward Island, near Corpus Christi. This base was located out on the gulf coast on an island. The island was connected to the mainland by a long bridge. This was not part of the main Corpus Christi Naval Air Station, but was a teaching facility for the radar maintenance for planes of the U.S. Naval Air Corps. To get to Ward Island, we'd travel around Corpus Christi Bay on the south side and keep driving, observing things there. Corpus Christi Bay was probably 8-10 miles across and very shallow, which I'll later describe. By being shallow, I mean not more than maybe

15-20 feet deep, but bigger ocean vessels could come into Corpus Christi because there was an area that was dredged all the way out of the deeper water.

We arrived at Ward Island and were assigned to barracks there to start our schooling in the repair and maintenance of Navy aircraft. We moved into our barracks, which were on stilts. Later on, in the course of our stay there, we would learn why the barracks were on stilts. In other words, we had a stairway up to the main floor and the stilts were about 8 feet high. The stilts were big wooden posts that held the barracks up from the ground, so that the crawling creatures couldn't get in. We did meet some other crawling creatures very soon in our stay. One incidence was when I opened my locker. There were probably 100 cockroaches in there! We soon found out that it was impossible to stay away from these crawling creepers. I would be stationed in Ward Island Naval Air Station for about 3 months, unless after each week's testing, you washed out. If you washed out 2 weeks in a row, you would be sent to the South Pacific to the sea.

Well, pride took over, and not necessarily dodging combat, but pride would carry you through as far as trying to maintain your status as progressing through the course. The laboratories that we worked in were fabulous for that day and age. They were filled with electronic equipment. We had gone through our first month at Chicago and our 3 months in Great Lakes, learning maintenance of electronic equipment (radar, radio, IFF, and different kinds of machines). Now we were exposed to a different set of gear ("gear" stands for equipment in Navy language). The "head" means the latrine in the Army, or the bathroom, for lay people. So, you did get acquainted with Navy language quickly.

The base was surrounded by high fences with barbed wire and was heavily guarded by Marines because of a lot of secret equipment that we were working with. In fact, at night when we would have to stand watch, we would have to carry a loaded 45., and were instructed to shoot first and ask questions later. One night when I was on watch, a couple of fellows who had gotten quite loaded with booze were able to somehow climb over the fence. I yelled, "Halt!" And then I yelled it again and fired into the air. I was just not able to shot at them. I explained later to the office in charge that I though I had seen something near the fence and I shot at it, but it was just nothing there. He said that was acceptable in the report. Later on, I was thanked by a couple of fellows when they found out who it was on watch, and they said they had gone to a party in town and had to walk all the way out to the base because there were no buses that time of night. I told them, "This time, okay. Next time, not so good."

Every day for many hours we would work in labs and at the end of the week they would test us on the machines. They would cut wires, and sometimes put tape over different connections so we would have to find out where the trouble was as far as the machine not working. One interesting machine was the IFF and that was "Identification, Friend or Foe." All of the Navy aircraft had these and you could tell most of the time whether it was a foe or friend by just adjusting some dials and pressing some buttons. It would respond in such a way that it would tell you whether the other plane had an IFF machine made by this country or not.

Later on, after I got out of the Navy, I got credit for this course at Augustana. The first month we worked in laboratories, which were loaded with equipment. The second month we started working in the aircraft. We got carried away one day. I guess I was a practical joker at that stage too. We got the same frequency as a local disc jockey in Corpus Christi and everyone would start talking. We would ask him questions and he was wondering where it came from, but he soon found out that it was at the Navy Base again. Apparently, he had had previous trouble. He just puts in a call to the captain, and the captain was right down there very soon to find out and check out who was there in the plane, causing the trouble. We got by with it, but we didn't test out our luck any further than that.

On weekend leave, we would go to Corpus Christi, which, at that time was 1/3rd Mexican, 1/3rd black, and 1/3rd white. Even if you went to the best restaurant in town, you would have cockroaches come across the table once in a while. People down there apparently just live with these little things. There were 2 hotels downtown with restaurants in them. One was a tall skyscraper, and the other one was a shorter one. And the story goes on. There was a Mrs. Pat Driscoll, that went to the restaurant in the smaller hotel and she didn't like the food. She said, "I will build a hotel larger than yours and spit on the top of your hotel." And she did proceed to do that. That's why those hotels were located that way.

There were some nightspots, but we were always under the gun as far as getting back to the base at certain times. It sure got hot down there. We were warned that if you were exposed to the sun too long, over 20 minutes, you might be burned very badly, and two of my shipmates were really burned around the neck. I'm sure that to this day they carry scars from being burned so badly. Another bad feature was people with fungus in their feet, or athlete's feet. One of my bunkmates got athlete's foot so bad that he had to go to the hospital and stay there for about 2 weeks. The skin literally peeled off his foot.

On Sunday mornings when we didn't have duty, we would go to our favorite spot and eat pancakes. That was a big highlight, because this small café made real good pancakes in town there. While I was at Corpus Christi, we had several big time stars come there and sing to entertain us. We had Bob Hope, Frank Sinatra, Mitzi Gaynor, and others. We had Harry James' orchestra and Tommy

Dorsey's orchestra as well. We also had a nice theatre, but it burned down while we were there, which caused a lot of trouble for everybody. Then after that, we had outdoor movies. In sports, I played with the Corpus Christi basketball team. We didn't have a football team. The basketball team would play against some other colleges around there, like Texas A&M and Texas University. I didn't get to play too much because there were a lot of really good players there, but I had fun being on the bench and getting in once in a while to play.

I was invited one night with a bunch of sailors to the home of some southern people and they had a dance out in their backyard. They had erected a large wooden dance floor, and we had a lot of fun that night. We got to talk to a lot of southern belles, but nothing serious. Probably the biggest event while I was there was the hurricane that hit, and I don't remember the name of it, but since then I have listened once in a while to hear it mentioned. That hurricane in 1945 was a bad one. Prior to the hurricane, we were able to board up all the windows of the barracks. We had to fly close to 1,000 planes out of Corpus Christi's main base and Ward Island. They were taken up to northern bases in Texas to preserve them. Some of the testing planes remained and we had to tie them down with large nylon ropes to withstand the pressure of the hurricane.

One thing about the hurricane is that we learned about it 36-48 hours ahead of time, so that gave us time to prepare. We had no idea how severe it would be but we found out later. We were told that we were in a good spot because the shelf of the gulf was not too deep, so that it wouldn't be like in the Galveston, Texas area, where the tidal wave can build up to 20 feet or more and wipe everybody out. This gave us some courage. As the hurricane approached, we got more prepared, and I remember one particular night when it reached the height of its severity with winds up to 130 miles/hour and constant rains that came in an avalanche and poured down on us. During that night I was stationed at the PX, which is the restaurant and shopping area. The electricity went out so we were all in the dark, and heard rumors that the roof of the hospital had blown off. We were worried about ourselves and people who went from place to place had strung up ropes from building to building so that you could hang on to the ropes in case of an emergency and get where you needed to go.

The rumors were really flying that Port Aransas, about 10 miles away, had been wiped out and that our bridge to the island had been wiped out. It was true. So, we were isolated that way. Then, since the electricity was gone, we had to eat ice cream. I have never eaten so much ice cream in my life. Over the next 24-36 hours, during the height of the hurricane, we got so sick of ice cream! We had to eat it because it was starting to sour. We slept on the bowling alley and there were the largest cockroaches I have ever seen in my life! They were almost 1 and ½ -2 inches long, and large beetles and a few snakes had gotten into the building, so it wasn't a pleasant experience overall.

It just really felt like we were all going to blow away any minute, and this kept up for 12-15 hours. As the storm tapered off, we were able to go out and see all the damage it caused. Also, we went to town later on after we prepared the base, and we found that they had yachts way up on Main Street. They had washed over the sea wall and were all broken up like matchsticks. Luckily, the bridge was temporarily repaired so that we could go to the city of Corpus Christi and back. On the base, the planes that were left were heavily damaged. The water was receding under our barracks. That's the reason that we had been on stilts, because we would have been washed out to sea if we had been on land. The water came up on the island.

The other big event that happened when I was at Corpus

Christi was that some of my friends had gone home on leave and they were coming back into the base at the main air station. As they were arriving, another Navy plane was taking off, and I happened to be looking out at the Corpus Christi bay at that time and all of a sudden there was a huge fireball, and both the planes crashed into each other! Approximately 22 fellows from our group were killed on the spot. Boats, sirens, and planes circling all over was the scene for the next 24 hours, trying to search for bodies and for other injured people. This was a real tragedy. We had a big memorial service for these people who were killed and all their flag-draped coffins were standing there. Everybody sang the Navy hymn and there wasn't a dry eye in the place.

While I was there in the 3rd month of the training program, we were taken up in planes to operate the radar equipment, and we were flown out over the gulf quite a ways. We had a couple of flights over to the West Coast to search for Japanese submarines, and we flew out several miles along the coast with PBY planes (that's a big flying boat). We would search with radar and learn how to use the equipment and repair it if anything happened to it. Then we would fly back to Corpus Christi. One time we flew with an SBD bomber (that's a dive bomber used by the Navy off aircraft carriers) and one of my friends challenged the pilot and said, "You'll never get me airsick." His name was Sheppe. He went to St. Cloud State prior to coming to the area down there. One of my other friends was Marette. The other guy was Bob Nelson. They're 3 guys we hung around with a lot.

On this trip with the dive-bomber, Sheppe came back and his face was just green. He had thrown-up the entire trip and the guys in the crew just laughed at him and said, "Now you'll never say that again to us." I soon learned what they meant, but I wasn't fool enough to open my mouth too wide. I went up in the air with them and we flew along the coast. It was beautiful. Then they started tipping the wings and rolling the plane. I did get dizzy and a little airsick, but not to bad. I didn't throw up, but he was kind to me. He said, "I just want to you feel the feeling that we have when we roll the plane." The difference is, of course, they were used to it. Anyhow, I got through that experience. At that time, we were traveling very fast for propeller-driven planes.

Another very big event was the surrender of Japan. The end of the war had come and we hadn't seen any combat, although we had been out over the coast watching for submarines. There was really a big celebration downtown in Corpus Christi. They let most of the guys from the base down there. There were big parties all over, and people were dancing in the streets! There was hope that you would get out of the service. Up to that time, you really felt you were in there permanently because there was no end to the war in sight. You kept hearing all the bad news out of the Pacific.

In the fall, I went to football games at the local high schools and learned to appreciate Texas football. The stadiums are full. They would have 15 or 20,000 at a high school football game! The Corpus Christi air base had a football team, too. We got to know a few of the players, but I wasn't allowed to try out for it because we were too busy in our work. Also, we took trips to Matamoras, Mexico and back. Matamoras is just across from Brownsville. Actually, one time I hitchhiked down there and I got just as far as Arlington, which now has a baseball team, the Texas Rangers. Then I had to hitchhike back, and I made it back to the base by midnight. I rode the back of a big laundry truck all by myself.

Then fall changed to winter, and Christmas came. That was some experience, because of the large number of servicemen who wanted to get back to their hometowns. We called the airlines, and we called the railroad stations, but everything was filled up. There was no way we were going to get back to Minnesota and South Dakota. Finally, a fellow named Wharton bought an old car, and the one problem we had was that the heater wasn't working. But the car was running, and we were able to get enough gas to get going, and so we traveled from Corpus Christi.

First off, we stopped in Iowa. We stopped at the home of one of the fellows there. By then, we were really freezing, even with our dress blues and P-coats on. We had a meal there and we wanted to get going again. We let off one of the fellows at a farm place there. There was already 12 inches of snow on the ground and it was about 14 below 0. We were really freezing, especially our feet, even though we had 2 or 3 layers of socks on and heavy boots. Then they got the brilliant idea of heating some bricks! They got these bricks almost red-hot, and then they put them on the floor of the car. We put our feet on them so that we could travel to Council Bluffs, where Wharton (the one that owned the car) was let out. Graciously, he let us take the car further up to Worthington, MN, where another guy was let out. He kept the car, and my folks met me at Worthington and took me back to Dell Rapids, South Dakota.

I spent about a week in Dell Rapids on leave. Of course, it was a very enjoyable week, because as a member of a pastor's family, there were a lot of Christmas services and so forth to attend. And also, my fiancée, Mary, was there. We saw a lot of each other during that week. We went to some shows and so forth. Then the time had come to go back to Corpus Christi. The return trip went much better because the weather was a little nicer. We made it all the way back, and this guy, Wharton, sold the car. Wharton was a red-haired guy and so was Nelson. Nelson was from Minnesota. There was another fellow from Twin Lakes, and another fellow from St. Cloud. In all, there were about 6 of us in the car, which wasn't too roomy. But, then when you were in the Navy, you didn't have many clothes to take along. We tied some things on the roof. His car was a lifesaver for us to get home and back.

Shortly thereafter, we graduated from Corpus Christi and became 3rd class petty officers. They changed our names from radio technicians, or RT 1st Class, to 3rd Class Petty Officer with 1 red stripe on your arm, and it was called AETM 3C, which meant Aviation Electronics Technician's Mate, 3rd Class. We were noncommissioned officers, in other words. We then proceeded to Philadelphia. Again, we took the train, but this time it was a much better train. We arrived in Philadelphia downtown, and then boarded a bus.

Two events that I forgot to mention were the fact that my brother Olin got married to Mavis Heeren while I was in Texas. They got married at the Dell Rapids Lutheran Church and were married by my father, Pastor Odland. So, I didn't get to that wedding. There was no way I could get leave for that. The other thing was the wedding of my brother Paul. That was held in Bucyrus, Ohio, to Barbara Ruhl. Everybody was there apparently but me. I was unable to get there from Texas. By now, my brother Olin was stationed in Virginia Beach, Norfolk, VA, in the Navy there, having come back from the Pacific after 17 months of duty. Also, as I previously mentioned, now he was married and Mavis lived with him near the base in Virginia Beach. My brother Paul had finished medical school, the 2-year program, at South Dakota University, and the Navy program, and now had been transferred in the Navy program to Temple University in Philadelphia.

Now it's 1946, the spring months. I was stationed at the naval air station north of Philadelphia, about 15 miles from the suburbs of Philadelphia. That was our sleeping quarters, and we also received breakfast and evening meals there. They had good recreation facilities and there was really good duty. Every day the bus would load in the early morning hours and go to Johnsville Naval Air Modification Unit, which was a factory located about 20 miles east of the naval station where I slept and ate. We would arrive every day at the Johnsville plant and there were about 100 Navy personnel stationed there. We were up on the 2nd floor of a huge factory, which was run almost totally by civilians.

Every day we would have to walk through the plant to get to our special station, which was on the 2nd floor, almost like a balcony. Up there we would work on Navy equipment, things such as new radar equipment that we had never seen before. This was also the first time that I worked on televisions. The televisions were extremely small, 5 inches square, maybe. At that time they were going to be used for battle plans that you could see by periscope with a camera, and could see in the distance across the battlefield. The latest radar, which was really something new, was going to be put into B-17 bombers. We called them pregnant B-17's. That's because the belly of the B-17 was bulging out with this huge reflector underneath the surface and was covered by fiberglass. We helped install these with the civilians and tested them out. Then we would fly over the east coast of the United States and test out the radar.

Radar is a lot like television in that the further away you get, you have to have a high antenna, so that if you fly a B-17 up at 15 or 18,000 feet and use that as an antenna, you can see the whole coast of Chesapeake Bay up to New York, which was unheard of at that time. Down below us was the whole coast of New England or Washington area, and it was frightening to begin with because it was so accurate. Also, we were exposed to the first jets. Prior to this time, all aircraft except for the German's had been propeller-driven, and the Germans, near the end of World War II, had developed some jet planes. Propeller planes had a tough time dealing with them. The planes we had to deal with in the Navy aircraft were F8F, F4F Corsairs, and F6F Hellcats, and we helped install the equipment in them. The place where we lived was Willow Grove Naval Air Station, north of Philadelphia.

Here they had basketball courts and different things. I learned there to mix with some blacks that were very nice fellows, especially one who was 6 foot 5 inches, and an excellent basketball player. We had a team that did real well. One day we went into the Mess Hall and there was a white chef there who came up to our table and stated to the black fellow to get out of there. We told them that if he leaves, we all leave, and several of us whites went out with him. But, we found out later that this chef was a Southerner and he had not learned very faithfully that desegregation in the services had just begun and that we were allowed to go anyplace with the blacks.

Back to the Johnsville plant. Our bit project now that the war was over was to outfit F6F Hellcat fighter planes to be flown by radio control into the atom bomb experiment down in Bikini Atoll, in the South Pacific. They were starting to promote whether or not we would go there as Navy boys and help the project. They built it up real well that we could be not too far from the atom bomb experiment and that we could watch it through specially designed glasses from the ship and see how our planes performed when the bomb went off. They made it very attractive. They would give us a $1,000.00 bonus if we would stay in the Navy until September and take part in this experiment. Fortunately, because of the time of year, I was more attracted to going back and getting out for football and getting back to Augustana or South Dakota University in the fall of 1946. I wanted very much to continue my education, so I turned down this offer.

This was one of the best choices of my lifetime because many of the fellows did volunteer to go just to get the money, and I guess they increased the amount of money because not too many volunteered, up to $3,000.00 each. In those days, this was big money. Many of the fellows who did go to Bikini Atoll for the atom bomb experiment really regretted it later on in life. As we know now, a lot of those fellows have had radiation trouble and developed leukemia and other fatal illnesses. Personally, I don't know of anybody that this happened to, as what their name was, but I know some of the group that I was in did volunteer.

Some crazy things happened at Johnsville plant. They had a big roof, and when it got warmer in May of 1946, we would go up there and get well suntanned. The captain of the base was bored to death now. He had been overseas and now he had this base to take care of, and he would fly his glider every day whenever the weather was good. When we were sunning down below, he could spot us with his spyglasses. He would come down and try to identify us but nobody would give him any information, so he never got anywhere. But he was goofing off just as much as we were. Also, the thing that alarmed us about him was that he and his Lieutenant Commander cohort would rob the base of equipment. Considering it to be surplus equipment, they could take it off the base and sell it. They got by with it because we couldn't protest in those days. We just went along with it, knowing that some of the equipment was missing.

There was another thing we would do, which was sort of dangerous, but we somehow got by with it. Three or four of us would grab one of the jeeps and we were pretty good with electronics. We would get it to start without a key and we would take it over to the nearby swimming pools where the civilians were. We had a ball there, swimming around with some of the local people and sun tanning and so forth. Then when we would get back to the base, we would put the jeep back where it was, and we got by with this several times.

As far as other entertainment was concerned, we would get leave and go to Washington and New York. While in Washington, we went to some dances. It was hard to get any drinks there so then you would have to bribe a taxi cab driver to go and get a bottle for you. Then we would have our little parties. And after that, go to a dance. I can remember at one particular dance we went to, it was probably something like 10 girls to 1 guy, because at that time Washington was loaded with office girls during the war and after the war, and probably still is. We had a real good time. Nothing serious went on except about 4 of us walked 4 girls home that night. We forget to check on the taxicabs and everything, and we got out to the outskirts of Washington. I don't know how many miles we walked.

All of a sudden, we called for taxis and found out they had all stopped going after 1:00 a.m. So, we had to walk back to our hotel. We got back there about 3:00 in the morning. The next day or two, over the weekend, we would tour Washington. Here we would experience one particular event that was not so nice. We went up to the top of Washington Monument with 2 or 3 of my shipmates, and while up there I got quite violently sick. The elevators were just jammed with people, so I had to walk down those 2 or 300 steps to get down to the base and then went down to the bathroom and sort of heaved my guts out.

The next trip we took was to New York City. We went to the top of the Empire State Building and toured downtown New York and stayed there for a couple of days. The next weekend trip that we took while in Philadelphia was over to Atlantic City. We went to a dance there on the steel pier, where they have the Miss America pageant, or did for a long time. That's an interesting place. At this particular big dance, they had Claude Thornhill and his big time dance band. Of course, I just loved his music. We met with several girls and danced with girls that we never knew before, but we had a good time. Then we had to go back to the Navy base. The nice part of that was that it was out over the Atlantic Ocean, and the breezes would be coming through the open window and into the dance hall.

One rather bad experience I had while in Philadelphia was due to my young age and being quite naïve at the time. Wharton, Marette, Sheppe, and me went to the Philadelphia downtown bar. It was called the Philadelphia Bar. I am telling you this because I think I learned a lot of lessons that night. There was a Navy father of a chef who was standing by the bar. We went up and stood by him and he said, "The drinks are on me." He just had gotten news that his son was safe and he was on his way home from the South Pacific. He hadn't heard from him for a while. So, he would pay for all the drinks.

Up to that time, I had never had any free drinks given to me. This developed into a contest between Wharton and me. Several of the other guys dropped out very soon, but they kept pouring straight shots and double shots of straight whiskey with a beer chaser, and they kept on setting them up for us and we kept downing them, just down the hatch. By the time I was through, I had had 13 shots (1 oz shots) and Wharton had had 17 shots, so he won the contest. We drank this booze so fast that we didn't realize what was coming. I was pretty safe and sane at that particular time, but the alcohol hadn't caught up with me yet. All 4 of us walked to the door and we were going to go over to the USO across the street. As I came to the door, I suddenly was starting to feel it and became somewhat dizzy. With the fresh air outside, we finally made it over to the USO.

One of my buddies was saying that I was trying to really talk to one of the girls behind the counter that was in the USO troop. She was sort of sick and tired of me. But anyhow, later on, they took me back there a week later and showed me who it was and I couldn't believe it. She was homely as a mud fence! But, at that time, with all the influence of alcohol, she looked like the Queen of England. Anyhow, we didn't last very long there and we were dodging SP's (Shore Patrol). So, finally, Wharton and I went outside and all 4 of us were in sort of bad shape, but 2 guys were better. We sat down next to the building. We could see other Navy personnel coming by and saying, "Those poor saps." Somehow, 2 or 3 of the guys got a hold of us and they loaded us on the bus and got us back to the base. We were then able to get into the base and get to bed. That was on a Saturday night, and I think we slept a day and a half. When we woke up on Sunday, it was headaches galore. I told myself this would never occur again at this particular level. Knowing what I know now, as a doctor, I'm sure that we were very sick that night. We were probably closer to death than anything.

On the brighter side, while I was in Philadelphia, my brother was going to Temple University Medical School. This provided some extra experiences, too. Barbara and Paul were married now. They lived in an apartment on the 2nd floor in Germantown. Germantown is a suburb on the north side of Philadelphia. I learned how to get there from the base when I had liberty and I slept overnight a couple of times. While I was there, I would walk up to Germantown Main Street and walk around there and around the area. Also, while I was there, Barbara and her sister Virginia took Paul and I out to some relatives of Barbara's, out in the Skulkill River area, and that was beautiful. That's in the west part of Philadelphia. There is a large park there.

We spent the evening at a house of Barbara's relatives, and we were singing Irish songs by the piano. It was really a beautiful experience. I also remember that while we were there, we went to a church because my brother Paul was singing base with a quartet of medical students, and they were very good. One song that they would sing was "Summertime," and it was very pretty because one of the medical students had a high tenor voice. Later on, they made a record of this, and it was really good. At this time Paul was in the Navy in the B-5 program in medical school and he was a senior.

While I was in Philadelphia, we went to shows. One particular show we went to see was "Harry James and the Band," and there was a singer there that sang "It's the Talk of the Town." It was the hit of the country at that time. Also while in Philadelphia, Jean Crane, the movie star, came to our base and she had been in the show "State Fair." That was a popular show at that time. Also, a couple of times we had occasion to go to the Sunny Brook dance hall where Harry James and Tommy Dorsey were. We saw some of the big bands. That was fun because I had heard radio broadcasts from those areas before.

Then in the spring of 1946, my brother Paul graduated from medical school. He got his MD degree. He was the first of the 3 Odland brothers to get their M.D. degrees. There was another fellow, named Stenberg, who was there from Sioux Falls, South Dakota, and believe it or not, his nickname was "Stinky." It's a nickname he carried through South Dakota University and also Temple. His dad was a doctor in Sioux Falls. I believe he was a dentist. His mother and dad brought my mother out to graduation so I got to see her then. My mother and I and the Stenbergs went to graduation at the Temple Assembly Hall. It was very impressive. Shortly after that, my brother Paul was shipped out with Barbara toward the west coast, and they ended up in Long Beach, California at the Long Beach Naval Station. This is where he would be for a short period of time before having to go on a Navy ship out to sea.

During the spring of 1946, I had a leave to go back home by train. It was only a week, so I didn't have too much time to pick it out, but I went to the Navy PX and they had diamond rings and so forth there. I did pick out a nice diamond ring. It was a single diamond with small diamonds on the side, for about $75.00, which was hard to come by. I had to save up money for it because my salary at that time was $120.00 a month. Then I went down and talked to some Navy pilots and they stated that they would be willing to try to arrange a cross-country flight for me, but they said they could only take me one way. I would have to come back by train. So, here I was, flying with a Navy pilot in a SPD dive-bomber, which was the only thing available.

He had to go down to Florida for some errand, so we went to Florida first. He said that it wouldn't take too long, and it didn't. When we got to Florida, he landed at Pensacola Navy Air Station, and then shortly thereafter we took off again and we flew to Omaha, where he had some other errands to perform for his captain, and this worked out fine. He let me off and I had to take the train home from Omaha. I could only go to Sioux City from Omaha, and then I took the bus from Sioux City to Sioux Falls. There, I was met by my father, who took me to Dell Rapids, and I spent a week there.

One evening, and I can't remember the exact date, I gave the engagement ring to Mary Margaret, nicknamed "Dude." She accepted it and we had a great time that night. Then after that particular week, I can't remember too much else that happened, but that was the big event. I took the train back to Philadelphia and was getting anxious to get out of the Navy. Finally, my orders came and stated that I would be discharged at Bainbridge, Maryland Naval Base. Prior to being discharged, they would really go over you physically and also mentally, and try to get you to re-enlist. I would have no part of that. None of my Navy buddies that I knew did enlist again. So, at Bainbridge I was able to get my "ruptured duck." It was a little yellow thing that showed you had been discharged honorably from the Navy. You also got papers and so forth. Then, you were given fare to get home.

CHAPTER 6

THE AUGUSTANA VIKING

Do you not know that in a race the runners all compete, but
only one receives the prize? Run in such a way that you
may win it. Athletes exercise self-control in all things; they
do it to receive a perishable wreath, but we an imperishable
one. So I do not run aimlessly, nor do I box as though
beating the air; but I punish my body and enslave it,
so that after proclaiming to others I myself should
not be disqualified.

(1 Corinthians 9:24-27)

I took the train and arrived home. I believe it was July 6th, 1946, a free person to do as I pleased. There wasn't too much left of summer, so I did work at Morrell's for a month or 6 weeks. Then I had to make a decision about school. By now, Dude finished her junior year of college at the University of South Dakota, majoring in Sociology. I would make some trips down there to look it over, and really was waiting and hoping that I could go back to South Dakota University because I already had connections with the basketball coach. I hoped that I could play football there, too.

I met with Rube Hoy, the basketball coach, and he was glad to welcome me back. He said right out that he was hoping I could come back and play for him. When I got home from one of these trips, my father sat down with me and said, as he looked at me very sternly, "You're not going back to South Dakota University, you're going to Augustana." My 2 sisters and my 2 older brothers had all gone to Augustana. My sister Maurine had been there for 3 years and got a teaching certificate. My sister Eunice went 2 years and got a teaching certificate. Olin had graduated in 4 years, and Paul graduated in 4 years as well.

I could understand my father's viewpoint a little because he was such a strong supporter of Augustana. He had gone out on financial drives to help the college. My uncle had formerly been President there. I did go ahead in August of 1946 and hitchhike to Northfield, Minnesota to look at St. Olaf College. I stayed overnight with my cousin, David, there at the Granskous. My uncle, Clemens Granskou, was President of St. Olaf at that time and he encouraged me to come there. I toured the buildings, especially the Science Building, because I was interested in science. The only way to get up there at that time was for me to hitchhike, and I did that.

When I got back, I really was quite impressed with St. Olaf and wanted to go there, too. It was a very hard decision to make, but my dad cut that off pretty fast. He said, "We can't afford you going to St. Olaf." It's funny how your future can be affected somewhat by which college you go to, but I really feel at this point if I had gone to St. Olaf, I probably would have been a minister. If I went to South Dakota University, I would continue in Pre-Med and get into medical school there. But, my brother Olin was going to assist as football coach down at Augustana voluntarily with Lefty Olson and some of the others who would return from the war.

So, I got caught up in the spirit and worked at Morrell's, and then finally I quit there just before school started and went out for pre-season football practice at Augustana. I registered as a sophomore at Augustana, and got credit for the Corpus Christi electronics courses to apply to my science. At South Dakota University, I had had straight A's, but now I was embarking on a different program. I was more mature, also knowing that I wanted to either go into the ministry or be a medical doctor.

I returned from Bainbridge, Maryland, where I had been discharged from the U.S. Navy, and I returned to a house full of people. By now, my brother Paul and his wife, Barbara, were in California at Long Beach Naval Hospital where he was interning. My brother Olin and his wife, Mavis, were in

Dell Rapids at the parsonage. Mavis was pregnant with Cynthia, who was born the 28th of November 1946, at Dell Rapids. Eunice, my sister, was living in the parsonage with Donald G. Aucutt, her husband. They had been married since 1943. They had with them a son, Donald Michael, who was born on January 31st 1944. Mother and Dad, of course, were there. By now, Maureen was living on the farm and she had the 2 girls, Barbara and Gloria. Barbara was born in 1941 and Gloria in 1942. They weren't at the house too much, but they did drop in and out as needed.

This was the picture I saw when I came home from Bainbridge, Maryland; Mother and Dad, myself, Mavis and Olin, Donald, Eunice, and their young child, Donald Michael. That makes 8 total! With 3 bedrooms, it was sort of crowded and congested. When I came home, I was still going with Mary Margaret Hermanson, my fiancée. I was rather restless as I came back to Dell Rapids, as most veterans were. I had had some brief discussions with my father as to where I would go to school, either the University of South Dakota, or Augustana. When it comes right down to it, I think that issue was decided before I came home, because my father was a very strong supporter of Augustana and wanted me to go there.

We had a number of veterans, of course, who returned back home, and we would go out at night and maybe go to Sioux Falls or something on that order when I wasn't dating Mary Margaret. One Saturday night, which wasn't one of my better nights, the Beeler boys, that's the 2 Aasen twins and Don Bach, Dale Dunn, and myself, all graduates of DRHS, went to Jasper, Minnesota. My father had given me permission to take the car (which was still a 1940 Pontiac) because there was a shortage of cars at that time right after the war.

The Beeler boys had noticed that there was a great time being had every Saturday night at Jasper, so we took the trip of 18 miles across country to get there. In the downtown area there was a place called Gen's. That's where the young people gathered to dance and play the jukebox and drink beer and so forth. We had had quite a few drinks, but being the driver, I held back somewhat. Later on, when I came to Luverne as a doctor, I found 2 or 3 people that I had met that night at Gen's. Then later in the evening, we drove to Pipestone and met some young people that we later would meet at Augustana again. There was a place there that sort of was a nightclub, and we had a few more beers. As I said before, this was not one of my better nights.

On the way home from Pipestone, I was quite naïve about the operation of the car and didn't notice that it was starting to overheat. Dale Dunn was sitting in the front with me, and 3 other guys were in the back seat. They were out cold, tired and possibly a little inebriated. I'll have to admit that I had a few, too. As we came closer to the north of Dell Rapids, the engine finally stopped. What had happened was the fan belt broke and I hadn't read the gauges right. Somebody else came along and helped tow us into town, and I parked the car in front of the house. The car was really hot. At that time, all I thought was that the car would cool off and would be okay. The other guys went home from there. It was quite late, probably 1:00 in the morning, and I went up the stairs to bed.

When I woke up the next morning things were not too good because my father was supposed to go to Willow Creek for the morning service on Sunday morning and he couldn't get the car to go. He called his friend, Martin Jensen, and he took him out there, as he lots of times would. The upshot of the thing was that in the next day or two, we found that the engine of the car was ruined due to an over-heat that cracked the block. I had to walk around pretty humble those days for the next week or two. I kept waiting for my father to call me into the room and really blast me, but I'll have to respect him for this; he didn't say a word about this accidental problem, and that hurt more than if he had seriously disciplined me. I did apologize to him, but of course my brother and brother-in-law made the most of this problem. My sister-in-law, Mavis, never let me forget it. I think they thought I should be disciplined more and of course I expected that but it never happened.

Well, there really wasn't much time to get a job that summer. I did work out at the farm with Johnny Muller, helping him with harvest. I learned one thing at that time, that Johnny's in-laws and his mother and father really didn't respect him as much as they should, and they also would degrade him in his work. But I thought he was a fine farmer.

In the middle of August, I reported for football practice at Augustana College. Originally there were 75 present, actually close to 80. The head coach was Lefty Olson, who had come back from the war and really wasn't the same person as he was before he went to the service. His assistant was Bob Fitch, who was previously an All-American at Minnesota University. I learned a lot from Bob Fitch, about defensive play especially. There are quite a few players who quit those first 2 weeks because of the severe practices. We practiced 3 times a day to begin with the first week, and the 2nd week two times a day.

We were tired all the time and dehydrated most of the time because the temperature as I remember was around 96-102 degrees for a solid 2 weeks! The ground was dry. We were praying for rain because it would soften the ground when we fell. I found out right away that college football was a lot different than high school football. By the time the season was over, there were only 54 players on the team. So it certainly took its toll in injuries, people quitting, and so forth. The morale was high to begin with, but we had such a mixture of older and younger fellows. We had Don Allen, Don Halvorson, Benson, Okie, Haugejorde, Grotewold, and Sam Jensen. All of these fellows were from the 1942 championship squad. Here it was, 1946, and they were starting over again. By now, they were juniors and seniors, of course. Some of them panned out okay, but some of them had legs that were not as good as before. But when we started the season, they would be the prominent fellows because they had experience. It turned out to be a crazy, mixed-up season. Also, Bob Foy and Hanson were 2 of the previous veterans. By brother Olin was helping voluntarily as an assistant, and Ray Sandvig was doing the same.

Then school started. At that time football season, as far as regular games, would not start until about a week after school started. After school started, we had only 1 practice a day. Nasier Salem came out for scrimmages and helped coach also, and he was very good. He used to coach at Sioux Falls Cathedral, which is now O'Gorman. I was slated to play tackle on the right side of the line and end, but because of the veterans, wasn't going to play too much to begin with. We also had a bunch of fellows who came back from the service who hadn't gone to college yet, like Alan Hopper, Don Kruck, and Jim Hassan. A lot of these guys were stars at Washington High during their glory years. They also had the Hirsch brothers from Sioux City. My closest friends, besides some of the veterans, were Jacque Schmidt, who had also played in the state tournament against me, and Lloyd Dobratz and Bob Christensen, who came from Minnesota.

I also got along quite well with some of the veterans because my brother Ole played with them in 1942. I was carrying a heavy schedule (Pre-Med). In Organic Chemistry, I was a lab assistant, and that's the only extra money I would get toward my education. I was in that position (chemistry lab assistant) for 2 years at Augustana. I was also taking Biology, German, and English, a fairly heavy load of about 18 hours. As I previously mentioned, prior to this time (or prior to going to the Navy) I had almost a straight-"A" average at South Dakota University, but now things got tougher. This was mainly because it was a tougher school you might say, but also playing football full-time wasn't easy.

As the season started, we had real high hopes. The first game was a 6-6 tie against Gustavus Adolphus. That was played in Sioux Falls before a large crowd. "Gustie," at that time, was almost a national champion in their division. I did get in and play about a quarter of the game, but found out right away that I was playing with the big boys. Gustavus had a big 260 lb. All-American tackle named Peterson (I think it was Vic Peterson). When I was in there, I had to play against him and that was murder. By now, I weighed about 214 lbs. And he weighed 260. After the game when we tied Gustavus, we thought we were on a roll because they were supposed to be very good. The upshot of the whole thing was that they went undefeated the rest of the season except for that tie, and I'll tell you more about our record.

It wasn't easy to see Mary in the fall of 1946 because I was busy with football season and we were on the road and so forth. We made a trip then to North Dakota State at Fargo, and the bus trip was really fun even though it was a long trip. We were able to stay a couple of nights up there in Fargo, take the bus back, and usually get back on Sunday. In Fargo, we met up with the North Dakota State Bison and had a good game with them. We lost by 1 touchdown. We then played Northern State at Aberdeen and I believe we lost by 1 touchdown again. Close games, but 2 losses. Then we played Morningside in Sioux Falls, and this was for Viking Days. Everybody was pretty hep on trying to win a game. But, again, we lost 14-0. I can remember that night because when we came off the field, some of the Augustana supporters would come up and slap us on the back and say, "You guys didn't do too good tonight." That sort of taught me about fans and their support. Here we were losing in a losing cycle trying our best to win, and they were sitting in comfort on the sidelines. But we had to eat the mud and play our game and still take criticism.

We went to Topeka, Kansas to Washburn University, and we spent 2 nights there. After we lost to Washburn, which was a much larger University of about 14,000 students, we were able to be invited to a party and really had a good time afterwards. That particular game, we lost 20-13 in a rather well played game in good weather and a beautiful stadium. Then, it was time to go to Hobo Day at Brookings and play SDSU. It was a nice Saturday afternoon and there was a capacity crowd. I was looking forward to playing. I believe the final score was 25-13, and we lost another one. There was one interesting thing that happened to me in that game. I was ready to go into the game in the 3rd quarter and was sitting by Lefty Olson, the coach. Augustana punted to a little guy from State and his name was Dudley Melichar. He came running toward the sidelines and lo and behold there was a big pile-up. His cleats came up and hit me in the face, actually injuring Lefty Olson's left shoulder and breaking my nose!

Of course, this was really an embarrassing thing to be sitting on the bench and get your nose broken. On the same play, there was a big tackle from South Dakota State that broke his leg. When I got back to Sioux Falls, I had to go to a Dr. Opheim (Warren Opheim's father). He just put his hands on my nose and pushed and pushed and pushed and finally the thing straightened out somewhat. Of course, my nose bled like it was going out of style. But, he was sort of crude, and unfortunately was the team doctor. The next week, we went to Northern in Aberdeen. I was slated to play more and they just put a bandage on my nose and ordered a special nose guard to put in front of the helmet. At that time, nobody wore nose guards or face guards except if you needed to for protection of a nose fracture or something like that. The nose guard was just an invitation in the 2nd quarter for one of the Northern boys to grab a hold of my nose guard and pull it down real fast and hard, and it just crunched my nose again. The second time was more painful than the first time.

The following week, we went to North Dakota U. and here again we had problems with penalties. We had 100 yards of penalties at half-time, even though we were leading 13-7. The 2nd half became a problem because by then we were running out of gas against a superior organization. North Dakota University, being a large school, beat us 20-13. That was a long bus trip home. We went right through Dell Rapids, so they dropped me off there on a Sunday. I just had to be back in school on Monday and get back into the routine of things.

Then the last game of the season came. That was with UNI, which was at that time called Iowa State Teacher's College, in Cedar Falls, Iowa. That was a long trip down there. They were the conference champions. It snowed during the game on Saturday afternoon. We really felt like we were in enemy territory and they took us apart. That had to be the dirtiest game I have ever played in, in high school or college football. They had some blacks on their squad, but they weren't necessarily the dirtiest. But they would pull a lot of stuff in the pile-ups that I had never seen before. I'm not going to enumerate those things right now. Pretty soon, it became a headhunting game and we were really buried score-wise. We ended up on the short end, 34-0. So, as I told you to begin with, our season was disastrous. I really learned a lot from the football season and had a lot of comrades in arms, you might say. We got to know the fellows pretty well, what you could do and what you couldn't do. We ended up with 1 tie and 7, losses and we were at the bottom of the conference, naturally. We had a lot of fellows returning for the next year. Some of the veterans would be with us, but they hadn't really panned out that well that particular year.

In the fall of 1946, Don Aucutt became coach at Garretson High School, and my sister Eunice moved with him over to Garretson. That became another thing that my dad was very interested in, going to Garretson to see football games in addition to Dell Rapids High School games. Of course, on weekends, he would try to follow the Augustana team. He was very supportive during our losses. That fall, Mary and I got along real well. We didn't see too much of each other, and she was going to be graduating as a senior in the spring of 1947. We did, however, see a lot of each other over Christmas vacation.

During the fall of '46, my brother Olin and his wife moved to Vermillion for his first year of medical school. My brother Paul was in the Navy taking an internship. He was stationed at Long Beach, and soon would be going to sea. He would be going to the north Pacific waters near Alaska and leaving behind his wife and young daughter, Judy. He would become a doctor on a Navy tanker and during that rough water he would become seasick for a long period of time. He lost many pounds during his tour of duty at sea.

Myself, I would be starting basketball. A lot of veteran players had returned to Augustana, plus 3 of us from Dell Rapids (Chuck Berge, Fred Lauer, and me). For me, it was a difficult change from what I was used to on the University of South Dakota basketball team before I went into the service. The coach at Augustana was Lefty Olson, and he insisted on everything having to be a programmed type of movement on the court. This was in contrast to a few plays that Coach Rube Hoy had at South Dakota U. There was a feeling on the basketball team that he certainly favored the local boys from Washington High at that time. I played some with the varsity, but didn't really get a very good chance to play and I found myself discouraged. I was able to play on the B-team quite consistently and some on the A-team, but then, after Christmas, we were going to have a game with South Dakota State at home. It happened during Christmas vacation that a bunch of us players got together from Dell Rapids and Dell Rapids St. Mary's. On that team was Sonny (Jim) Schmidt, who played and was a star at South Dakota State. So we knew quite a bit about his style of play, and he was a very good player. It just so happened that because we were going to play South Dakota State right after Christmas, that after practice one day during Christmas vacation at Augustana, Lefty Olson, the coach, called me into his office. He sat down behind his desk and he said, "Odland, I've got something here I want you to read."

It was totally embarrassing. He had a letter from my mother. My mother was quite a fan, and was very loyal to Augustana and Dell Rapids, and she had figured out in her own mind that if Fred Lauer and I would play in that game against South Dakota State, we could beat them because we had handled Sonny (Jim) Schmidt fairly well during our scrimmage squad games at Dell Rapids. I wish I could've saved that letter because the family joked about it many times in the ensuing years, about her being a "coach." It turned out that she probably was right in that we did lose a close game to South Dakota State, and Sonny (Jim) Schmidt, who was their star player, ran wild during that game.

About the middle of January, I decided I had had enough, and so did the other two Dell Rapids players. In the meantime, we had been playing some Y-ball and playing on a Dell Rapids independent team on the side, which was against the rules at Augustana. But they didn't know about it. We formed what we called the Dell Rapids Legion team and we were really mopping everybody up around the area (the independent teams). We played about twice a week, which was difficult with my college schedule. Fred Lauer, Chuck Berg, and myself left the Augustana team. It was just totally frustrating.

Later in February, we would come back and play at the Augustana gym against the Neuronian Society. This male society on the campus was composed of mostly basketball and football players and the entire present varsity basketball team was in that society. So, we scheduled a game against them, against the wishes of the college coach, and we packed the Augustana gym. The Dell Rapids Legion Team beat the Augustana varsity. When they published this in the paper, the coach, Lefty Olson, was quite mad at all of us. Later we became friends again.

We toured around and played a few games here and there. Later in the spring, about the middle of March (around Easter time), we played in the State Independent Team Tournament and we beat Alcester, Mitchell, and Aberdeen, I guess. We played Mitchell in the finals at the Corn Palace in Mitchell, South Dakota, and we beat them quite handily. We went on to the National tournament in Terre Haute, in southern Indiana. In the meantime, Mary and I had sort of a falling-out and things weren't going too well. We parted friends, and she gave back the engagement ring, because things just weren't working out, we didn't get a chance to see much of each other anyhow. We thought maybe later on we would get together again, but for the time being we were both too busy in our own colleges.

Then we made the big trip, with a lot of publicity, and the team went to Terre Haute, Indiana for the National Championship Finals of independent teams. At that time the tournament was sponsored by the American Legion. There were 8 teams left from the National Regionals, and we were one of them. Right off we met the eventual champions, from Mondovi, Wisconsin, which had a lot of Wisconsin varsity players on the team. We played them close and eventually lost by 2 points in the finals. They had 2 more games and the won them both to become the national champions.

We were able to win the consolation finals against a team from New York, and one from Dallas. Sunny (Jim) Schmidt was on our team since South Dakota State was through with their varsity schedule. He played center, Chuck Berg and Fred Lauer played forwards, and Phil Anderson and I played guards. The substitutes were Don Bach, Tom Merry, and Jiggs Merry. Carroll Sands was the manager, and the owner of Coast to Coast in Dell Rapids was the coach, pretty much in name only. Junior Phillips came along, too. After the games were over, we had sort of a wild time in a town called Brazil, Indiana, which was a nearby town. We survived and got home after that for Easter.

In the spring at Augustana, I finished my first year there and would take summer school. During the summer school, I would take the last year of German and American History, and a mathematics course. So by September I would be a senior in college. During the summer, I also held down a job on the side at Morrell's, cleaning in the smoke-bacon department. I would show up there every day about 2:00 p.m. and stay there until about 7:00 in the evening. I was able to do some studying on the side by finishing my work, which was quite unsupervised, and then studying, because we were going through the courses so fast.

Late that summer in 1947 I worked part-time at the beach in Dell Rapids as a lifeguard. During this time, Mary and I weren't seeing too much of each other. She was dating other fellows, and I was dating other girls, but I was pretty busy with summer school. Come the middle of August, it was back to football again, with a much better atmosphere prevailing. By this time, Bob Fitch had taken over as head coach and Lefty Olson was assistant coach. You could smell it in the air that it was going to be a much better situation this year.

I was back at Augustana in the fall of 1947 and went to preseason football practice. Prior to this, on January 25,

1947, Bob Fitch was appointed head football coach, and Lefty Olson, who had been coach at Augustana for 17 years, would now devote his full time to Athletic Director and assistant in football. During Lefty's tenure at Augustana with his football teams, he had a record of 80 wins, 29 losses, and 2 ties. Mr. Bob Fitch was the world champion at that time in the discus, and a former All-American football star at the University of Minnesota.

We again started out the season in a rather dismal fashion, but along the way we learned a lot of things. We went up to Gustavus Adolphus for the first game of the season and lost to Gusty by a score of 21-7, after leading 7-0 at the half. We played good defense, and fairly good offense as far as the line was concerned, but we had a lot of difficulty settling on a quarterback that would be consistent. Then we played Washburn University again at Topeka, Kansas and we lost 27-0. They were tops in their division for the year. We returned home to be edged by the University of North Dakota in a real close ballgame, 13-7, again leading at the half 7-0. We then went to Sioux City to play Morningside, which really had a good team. They had a quarterback named Callahan who was All-North Central, and we held on to beat them 14-7, for our first victory of the season.

Then, on a Saturday night, the big battle with South Dakota State and the evening of Homecoming came. This rivalry had become quite bitter over the years. Don Kruck and I were playing tackles, starting both on offense and defense. In those days, we had to play both ways. We were following the coaches' plans real well and were holding everything inside the tackles, and anything outside the tackles was supposed to be the end's and linebacker's responsibility on running plays. Early in the 4th quarter, we still held an edge, 13-12, in a Homecoming battle. Then everything seemed to go wrong.

The Jackrabbits exploded and finally ended up with a

32-13 victory, scoring 20 points in the 4th quarter. Afterwards, the coaches were blaming Don Kruck and I for not holding up our end of the bargain, but later on (on Monday or Tuesday), after looking at the films, they apologized and stated that it was the end's and linebacker's fault, not ours. One of the halfbacks for South Dakota State ran wild in the 4th quarter and he was running to the outside. We didn't make the adjustments, and about halfway through the quarter, the coach pulled both Don Kruck and I off the field and gave us the business, blaming us for some of the problems. It was after this disappointing loss that Don Kruck and his wife, Dinny, met Mary and I (who had our first date for the whole fall) and went to the Lemond's Café downtown with a bunch of other Augustana football players and their wives and girlfriends. We had dinner and a nice evening. Therefore, after a long cooling off period between Mary and me, we finally got back together and everything was very fine in the future from that time on.

The following Saturday, the Vikings nudged North Dakota State 13-7. This was also on the home field. At that time, the home field was on the campus next to what was the gym at that time, and at the present time this is a parking lot for several of the buildings. Today, Augustana has a practice field, but also plays at Howard Wood Field near the Arena. The climax of the football season came when the Norsemen unleashed all of their Norwegian vengeance and fury upon the previously unbeaten and untied Northern State gridders. The final score was Augustana 39, Northern 6. But then we couldn't stand prosperity and the Vikings lost to the North Central Champion again, called Iowa State Teachers (which is now UNI), 39-0.

Therefore, we ended the grid campaign with a record of 2 wins and 3 losses in North Central play, and an overall result of 3 wins and 5 defeats over the season, as that was the usual story of playing only 8 games per season. The later success in the season was probably attributed to the fact that we switched Chuck Okie from end to quarterback in mid-season. He was All-Conference at the end of the season, and that helped our offense. Scholastically, I continued to do well in the fall of 1947, and was also a lab assistant in Chemistry with my professor, John Froemke. I was taking Advanced Biology and Advanced Chemistry (organic and inorganic), and I was developing a double major in Chemistry and Biology. Also, I was still a member of the Gladstonian Social Society.

During the summer of 1947, I had moved into an apartment called "Ma Moon's," and to this day, I don't know what her first name was. Alan Tufteland (a good friend of mine from high school days at Dell Rapids) and I were roommates. This worked out okay because the bus line came by there, 1 block away, and took us to Augustana. Alan also had a car, and I would ride with him quite a bit. In some ways, this was not good because you missed some of the college life on campus, but really, I had all I could do between sports, music, and a tough schedule in Pre-Med, so that took care of most of my time. That summer Don Aucutt and I painted the Dell Rapids Lutheran Church. It's a granite structure with white wooden trim, and that was really almost too much to tackle. We painted the steeple using a double wooden ladder. It was really very risky and danger-ous, but we got by with it and did the job, and it was appre-ciated by all with very little pay to show for it.

One of the local night spots, called Don's Bar (of all things), was a place we would go after a full day's work with school and studying and so forth to have a couple of beers once in a while. Also, I frequently went home on weekends and usually took my books with me. That way, I could help my dad with some of the cleaning around the church, and also go to church and sing in the choir and so forth. Mary was now working at an insurance company

(New York Life Insurance) that had its offices downtown on about the 6th floor of the National Bank Building on Phillips Ave. Mary had graduated in the spring of 1947 from South Dakota University with a major in Sociology. This kind of work was a little difficult because of her lack of a business type of education.

In the fall of 1947, I started seriously thinking about medical school and applying to different locations. At that time, there was an overabundance of veterans coming home from the war and other students wanting to get into medical school. After the first year, in early 1948, I received notices of not being accepted at Minnesota University Medical School and Nebraska Medical School. I was disappointed, but then I got my acceptance from South Dakota University Medical School and Creighton Medical School in Omaha, Nebraska. Then I got my acceptance from Marquette Medical School in Milwaukee, Wisconsin. Prior to this time, I had conversations with Bob Collins, a graduate of Augustana whom I knew from previous times. He was presently a junior at Marquette Medical School and he encouraged me to apply there.

Also, I talked to Stan Devick, and he was finishing his sophomore year at the medical school in Marquette. They were both very positive about the school, and I became very excited about the whole situation. There were some rumblings, however (amongst my dad's brothers), that I would be going to a Catholic medical school. My father, however, didn't object at all. He thought it was a very fine school. Also, by then, my brother Paul was taking an orthopedic residency in Milwaukee at Wood's Veteran's Hospital, and I would be seeing him there later.

We had a wonderful Christmas that year because I knew that I was accepted at Marquette Medical School and was going there. I was really ready to focus on my future. My relationship with Mary became more solid and we were deeply in love. Her mother and dad and mine were real happy about looking toward our future as a couple. So, during the Christmas vacation of 1947, I proposed again to Mary after the previous cooling off period, and was successful in giving her an engagement ring, which she accepted delightfully. I, of course, had saved the ring because I thought this would eventually happen. We hadn't set a date yet, but were thinking about it.

During the winter of '47-'48, I played basketball on occasion, but was tapering off on my basketball activities because I was so busy getting ready for the end of the year when I would graduate from Augustana. After the first of the year, starting my last semester at Augustana, nobody could believe that I was already going to be graduating after a total of 2 and ½ years in college, counting summer schools. In the final analysis, I wasn't even listed as a Senior at Augustana because apparently the yearbook couldn't catch up with the fact that I was going through so fast.

During the spring of 1948, Mary, my fiancée, had been challenged to a new job. At that time there was a Mrs. Marvin Larson who was a teacher at Garretson High School. She taught classes, but she also was the vocal music teacher. Mr. Don Aucutt (my brother-in-law) was the principal there. Mrs. Marvin Larson (her first name was Doris) had to move because her husband was transferred. Don Aucutt prevailed on Mary to take the job as vocal music instructor and teacher at Garretson High School. She had to apply for a variance because she had not taken any education courses, but with the problems Garretson had finding somebody just for the remaining 2/3 of the second semester, they agreed to a variance. Her superintendent was Supt. Tandberg. To all of us, this was quite a challenge, and we were very, very surprised when she took the job.

Just to bring you up to date with the rest of the family, by now my father and mother were still living in Dell

Rapids and he was Pastor there. My oldest brother, Olin, was married to Mavis, and they had their second child in Omaha, Michael, in addition to their oldest girl, Cyndy. He was finishing his second year in medical school at the University of Nebraska in Omaha. My brother Paul was finishing his first year of orthopedic surgery residency in Milwaukee, Wisconsin. My sister Eunice of course, was living in Garretson with her husband, Don Aucutt. By now, they had 2 children, Donald Michael, and Richard Kincaid. My brother Paul had his daughter, Judy, and the 2nd child was Blair, who we called Paddy. My sister Maurine was married to John Muller and living on the farm, and by now had Barbara, Gloria, and Mary Ann. They were frequent visitors at the Odland household in Dell Rapids because we were so close, only 4 miles out of town to the north.

So, continuing on, here is Mary (Dude, her nickname) moving to Garretson and taking on the senior choir and soloists (the works, you might say), and living with a relative of hers, named Songstad. On weekends, I would take the train (yes, there was a train) to Garretson from Sioux Falls, since I didn't have a car, and we would spend a short time there and then drive to Dell Rapids together in her little car. During the spring of 1948, I was very busy taking examinations before graduation, and we were already making plans for the marriage. The date for the marriage would be August 1, 1948. Of course, the marriage ceremony would be at the Dell Rapids Lutheran Church, where my father was a minister, and he would be the minister in charge.

I graduated from Augustana, I believe, on June 4th, 1948. The problem was that I had not really finished college yet and I got a blank diploma. They knew, of course, I would be finishing after summer school. I had one more hurdle to go over. My final diploma, which was issued on the 14th day of August 1948, stated Bachelor of Arts degree, Cum Laude.

Actually, it should have been Magna Cum Laude, but they didn't give me credit for a couple of things that I did at South Dakota University, be that as it may. The diploma is signed by H.J. Glenn, minister at First Lutheran, and also President of the Board of Directors at Augustana, as well as the President of Augustana itself, Lawrence S. Stavig.

During that final summer, I took Physical Chemistry and Advanced Biology, and finished up some language requirements. I was doing all this while holding down a part-time job and going back and forth to Dell Rapids to see Mary during the summer. She was busy with showers and preparations for the wedding. However, the 4 of us did take a trip to Milwaukee. John, Alice, Dude, and myself, were hopeful that we would find an apartment. We stayed a couple of days there at the Abbot Crest Hotel across from the University of Marquette. Mary picked out a wedding dress at the Boston Store, downtown Milwaukee, and we made arrangements to get a 1-room efficiency apartment on about the 6th floor of the Abbott Crest Hotel.

This is what you would consider a residential hotel on Wisconsin Avenue, near the University of Marquette. We tried to find other apartments and were unsuccessful. We even contacted a Mrs. Wintergreen at Our Savior's Lutheran Church in south Milwaukee, where Pastor Reuben Gornitzka was located. Mrs. Wintergreen looked all over for apartments for us, but could not find one at that time. She stated that when we came back in late August that she would try again to find an apartment, but in the meantime we could stay at the Abbot Crest Hotel. The summer sure went fast, and it was a very eventful summer, as far as Mary and I were concerned. I was trying to just finish out my requirements at Augustana College and it was very tough to concentrate on the difficult course of Physical Chemistry. I think my friend and professor, Dr. John Froemke, had been my guardian angel and gave me an "A" in Physical

Chemistry. I felt that I didn't deserve it, but he felt I did. I'm sure in the end it helped me quite a bit as far as getting into medical school.

CHAPTER 7

THE MARRIED MAN

Set me as a seal upon your heart, as a seal upon your arm;
for love is strong as death, passion fierce as the grave. Its
flashes are flashes of fire, a raging flame. Many waters
cannot quench love, neither can floods drown it. If one
offered for love all the wealth of one's house,
it would be utterly scorned.

(Song of Solomon 8:6-7)

T hen the big day arrived. In those days, we didn't wear tuxedos. In fact, none of the wedding party wore tuxedos. But, I'll add this little incident that happened beforehand. I had become a very close friend of David Dexter, as he was my roommate my first year at college. I told my mother I was going to have him as Best Man. I'm sorry, but I was bucking tradition. There was no way that this was going to happen because my mother said I had to have the oldest brother as my Best Man.

I finally gave in to that suggestion and it was all right. Her statement was, "Long after your friend David Dexter and you have parted, your brother will still be around." That was true and it worked out fine. I asked my brother, Olin, to be the Best Man, and the groomsmen were John Hermanson (my future brother-in-law), David Dexter (my roommate in college). The ushers were Don Aucutt, my brother-in-law, married to my sister Eunice, and my other brother-in-law, John Muller, married to my sister Maurine.

On Mary's side, the Maid of Honor was Reefa Hannenberger. She was Mary's best friend through grade school and high school. The bridesmaids were Dorothy Hermanson, at that time, wife of John Hermanson, and Marjorie Erickson, married to one of my best friends, Dick Lindquist. She was a college sorority sister. The other attendants were Virginia Paulson, first cousin of Mary Margaret, and Harriet Whitney, who was a sorority sister of Mary Margaret. This completed the wedding party. The wedding was to be held August 1st, on a Sunday, at 7:00 p.m., 1948. My father, Pastor Ole Odland, would be the pastor in charge. Mary could probably fill-in some of the details very well and possibly in the future we'll leave some space for her to fill in some of the details of the wedding and so forth.

Her wedding gown was bought in Milwaukee, Wisconsin, at the Boston Store. It was very beautiful. In those days, as you can see from the pictures of the wedding, we all wore suits instead of tuxedos. Tuxedos were a special commodity. I wore a brown double-breasted suit with a gray and brown striped tie. There was considerable concern on that particular day because of the weather changing from a warm Sunday to possible rain showers. In those days, we didn't have extensive weather reports, but rain was predicted. This brought up the problem of having an outdoor reception in the back yard of the John Hermanson family.

However, after our beautiful wedding ceremony, the newly married couple and their friends and relatives all went to the John Hermanson residence for a wonderful post-wedding reception. It did not rain and all who attended had a very good time. At this point, I should have included a clipping from the wedding, which I'll come across some place, which would include all of the relatives who attended the wedding. After a beautiful wedding reception, the bride and groom (yours truly and his wife, Mary Margaret, called "Dude" for short) proceeded westward in the newly acquired car. The car was far from a new car, but was given by the parents of the bride. The car at that time was a 1937 Chevrolet, a beautiful black 4-door sedan, and had very few miles on it. It was almost a collector's item and it purred like a kitten. We proceeded south to

Sioux Falls on old Highway 77 and turned west. We had reservations at the Lawler Hotel in Mitchell.

A little sidelight is that John Hermanson Sr. was very particular about reservations and having everything done right. We just recently ran across a check that he had written for reservations at the Lawler Hotel. When we arrived, it was quite late at night and as I checked in, I didn't write Mary's name, and the clerk at the desk looked at her real peculiarly. Of course, the details of the honeymoon have to be somewhat deleted. The next morning we got up early because we had a long trip to the Black Hills. Our destination was Legion Lake in the Black Hills, near Custer. This particular group of cabins was on the side of a mountain overlooking a lake, and at that time was considered to be a tremendous trip.

Things like going to Hawaii and St. Thomas and Mexico and Acapulco and those things were unheard of at that time. Our country had just gone through a serious World War II, and also a serious depression, so funds were very limited. Certainly, in my case, I was almost flat broke. In the coming 4 years and even longer, a lot of my expenses were either funded by Mary working or my working on summertime jobs, as well as support of a great degree by John Hermanson, my father-in-law. Anyway, Back to the Honeymoon. We had our cabin in the Black Hills and stayed there about 4 days. We toured the Black Hills every day and took movies, which we still have. We even took horseback rides and about got killed, but anyhow survived. After 4 delightful days of honeymooning, we came back to Dell Rapids to open the gifts, as she was very interested. When home on vacations and after the honeymoon, most of the time we stayed at the Hermanson residence, because of lack of bedroom space at the Odland residence.

The rest of August 1948, I did some odd jobs helping out my father-in-law to get some expense money and get ready for medical school. In retrospect, I forgot to mention something that is of importance in regards to Mary's career. I did mention that she taught in Garretson, but I'm not sure that I mentioned she had the chorus and won Superior at the State Music Contest at Madison with her choral members. Getting back to medical school, I was accepted of course at Marquette Medical School, and we loaded up the car and went to Milwaukee about the 1st of September 1948. When we came to Milwaukee, we stayed at the previously arranged Abbot-Crest Hotel on Wisconsin Avenue, very near the medical school. This was going to be just a temporary arrangement for approximately 2 weeks so that we could find an apartment. Those were pretty hectic days, and I believe Mary's mother and father tried to help us find an apartment. In addition to this, we found some help through the church that we went to, Our Savior's Church, a Lutheran church in the southern part of Milwaukee. The pastor there was Reuben Gornitzka.

After a couple of weeks, we finally found an apartment and moved all of our life's possessions to this apartment with some help form the in-laws, and settled at 7605 West State Street in Wauwatosa, Wisconsin, a suburb of Milwaukee. We had an apartment over the 1st floor; in other words, we were on the second floor, an efficiency apartment in the back of the apartment building. In front, were some neighbors of course, and down below was a radio store. This was right downtown Wauwatosa. The business section was small, but there was a grocery store and a bank and a park and a little river going through behind our apartment.

We had some noisy neighbors on the 3rd floor above me, which made it difficult for studying sometimes, as they had some children there. Our back windows toward the south of the apartment, including our bedroom and our living room, overlooked the railroad tracks. What's so bad about that? Well, I'll tell you. The railroad tracks were the main line for the Milwaukee Railroad, both freight and passengers from Milwaukee to Minneapolis. About the first 2 nights we stayed there, I didn't think we could possibly stay, and found out why the apartment was available. After the first 2 nights, we hardly ever heard the trains again, although they were there. You could hear them coming from at least 6 or 8 blocks away and getting louder and louder and louder and finally shaking the curtains and shaking the walls of our apartment!

This particular year, we had very few visitors. At least, they didn't stay very long. Then, to help out with expenses, Mary went to work at a big Dodge distribution company. This company was located on West Wisconsin Avenue and she had to take the streetcar to work every day. The streetcar at that time had a station right behind our apartment, and that would go by the tracks across the main valley near the Miller Brewery Company, and had a real high trestle bridge. This was really a scary thing to look out over the side of the streetcar, but this is the way she traveled every day to work.

She had a job working for a Vice-President of the company. This Vice-President really didn't have anything to do, so she had to make work. She tried her best to make work so that his job would seem important. But also, he didn't care if she typed my term papers and my papers for medical school, and she did this frequently on the job. Her salary at that time was very acceptable, and did help us defray some expenses. In addition to that, I had help from the GI Bill of Rights after being in the Navy, and this took care of some of the tuition and so forth, but I had to pay for books.

We had quite a few friends in Milwaukee, both from medical school, and also our neighbors. My brother Paul arrived one year after we were in Milwaukee to start his residency at the VA Hospital in Orthopedics. I think previously I had stated that he arrived at the same time, but that's not true. Of course, I have to tell you something about medical school. The normal college undergraduate school's load would be 16 credit hours/semester, or approximately 30 credit hours/year, and to graduate, around 100-125 semester hours. In medical school your load is approximately 24-26 semester hours. All of a sudden, we as medical students had to shift gears and put in 8-9 hour-long days at school, plus every evening studying.

In September 1948 after orientation at Marquette University Medical School, we were given our classes and our partners for different classes. The real big course in the first year of medical school is Gross Anatomy. Gross Anatomy is from 8:00-12:00 every day, 6 days a week except for holidays, all through the school year. This is a course in which you are required to read a book called, "Gray's Anatomy" from cover to cover, which consists of about 2,000 pages of detailed anatomy. In addition to this, we had a laboratory book to follow (which was almost as thick as "Gray's Anatomy") for the dissection of the human body, which was a cadaver.

A cadaver is either a donated body or an unclaimed body that is taken from the morgue and soaked in formaldehyde tanks for a considerable length of time so it's preserved. There were 4 of us assigned to each body, 2 on each side. My 3 other partners were Walt Parmley, Ben Strehlow (who was 10 years older than I was), and Jack Brown (who was 6 years older than me). Each day, we would come and dissect, and read and dissect. Eventually, through the entire first and second semesters of the first year of medical school, we would cover the whole body. In addition to this, we had a course in Histology, which was very tough, and that was the microscopic analysis of tissues of the body. The third course was Biochemistry, and even though I was a Chemistry Major out of Augustana, it was very tough. Our teacher for this course was Armand J. Quick, M.D. He was the doctor who, through his research, developed the "Prothrombin Time."

One of the other professors of biochemistry was Dr. Laskowski. Our teacher in Anatomy was Walter Zeit and Weston Gardner. Off hand, I can't remember the name of the professor who taught us Histology. Our class, to begin with, was made up of 104 students. About 50% were Catholics, 40% Protestants, and about 10% Jewish (mostly from New York). We had students from all over the country, California to New York, because it was a private Catholic medical school. At the time I was in Milwaukee at the School of Medicine, and the undergraduate school of Marquette University was around 16,000 students. The University of Marquette was smaller than the University of Wisconsin, the state school, but our medical school class was larger than theirs.

Every day we had 8 hours of full class work and laboratory work with no time to study, so all of the studying had to be done in the evening. The noon hour was a lunch in the basement of the medical school. The medical school was on 16th street, just off Wisconsin Avenue in Milwaukee, Wisconsin. Sometimes I would take the streetcar from Wauwatosa down to the medical school, but most of the time would drive. Marquette is on a hill overlooking downtown Milwaukee. You can take Wisconsin Avenue straight down a gradual hill, all the way to Lake Michigan. I'm sure I was a very boring character to Mary, my wife, during medical school (at least the first 2 years as we had to constantly study). Our only entertainment was on weekends when we would go to a double feature movie someplace in Milwaukee.

Getting into late-October, I was very discouraged because grades weren't coming my way and Biochemistry was very difficult. At that point, I almost considered leaving medical school. Possibly, without encouragement from Mary, I would have done that. But when I went back to school after a big test where we got low grades, I found out that everybody else did, too. Almost nobody got any grades above a "C" because the professor wanted to wake us up and get us charged up to go further. Of course, we did have some parties to go to, that is, medical school fraternities and initiation parties and so forth. I was a member of the Alpha Kappa Kappa medical fraternity, but didn't live in the house. I lived in my own apartment with Mary, of course. There was another group, sort of the wilder group, called the Phi Chi's. We went to both fraternity houses and had some parties once in a while. After all, we had to loosen up after all of the studying.

A typical day would be to get up early and have an early breakfast, leave for the medical school and get there at 7:45, and start classes. Classes went from 8:00 until 12:00, off until 1:00, back on from 1:00 until 5:00, and then home. After supper, I would usually lay down for a 1-1 and ½ hours and then get up and usually study until 2:00 a.m. Then I'd wake up and go around again. Mary used to say that she knew my back very well as she watched me study.

Shortly after we arrived in Milwaukee Mary got a job at the Dodge distributorship garage. I had the GI bill to cover tuition and books, and I had saved it for this reason. We were allowed to save it in undergraduate work and use it for medical school. Of course, we didn't make our living expenses, so John Hermanson, my father-in-law, kindly helped us out. We, of course, had to stay in Milwaukee during Thanksgiving, but were able to get home at Christmas. At Christmas we were able to drive home and actually drove all night. This was the Christmas of 1948, and we had an old 1937 Chevy, which didn't have too many miles on it and was in good shape, but we had problems on the way home.

First, you have to understand that there were no interstates. We got to Lacrosse by Highway 16 from Milwaukee, and then we drove down the southern way through Rushford and all of those towns (Caledonia, Mabel, Spring Valley) on our way to Austin. However, we got stalled at Rushford at approximately 12:00-12:30 at night, on a Saturday night. Fortunately, we were stalled at –12 degrees, right at the edge of town. I was able to get downtown and talk to somebody there, and lo and behold they called a garage man and he did come and tow the car to the garage. We had to have the gas line cleaned out because it had frozen. We continued on our way after giving the fellow, I believe, $5.00. He was very grateful.

We then drove to Dell Rapids and arrived at approximately 7:30 a.m. and John and Alice, my in-laws, were eating at the breakfast table, and they were literally shocked when we walked in the door. We took 16 of these trips during those 4 years, back and forth to Milwaukee. It was really ironic as we came through Luverne, Minnesota, we would drive down Main Street at that time, which was the old highway, and stop at Long's Restaurant on the corner of Kniss and Main, and possibly have a cup of coffee and a sandwich or something. I noticed at that time it was a very nice looking town. Otherwise, I had never really been to Luverne except for the trips to and from medical school.

Of course, Christmas was a big thing with both the Odlands and the Hermansons, so we had celebrations both places. By that time, Dr. John Hermanson and his family lived in Valley Springs and they would come to these things too. Of course, after Christmas 1948, and New Years 1949, we traveled back to Milwaukee. Here Mary continued with her job and I went back to medical school. The second semester came and we continued with Gross Anatomy and then picked up Neuro Anatomy, and finished our Biochemistry in the first semester. We also added a second semester of Histology and a second semester of Gross Anatomy in addition to the Neuro Anatomy. Neuro Anatomy was taught by Dr. Fox. Medical school was very interesting. I found it quite easy to study long hours to achieve a purpose.

In the spring, we would go on picnics with Jack Brown and Eleanor, and Ben Strehlour and his wife Katherine. One of the sad things that happened was that Katherine had a mastectomy for cancer of the breast. Jack Brown had grown up in Milwaukee, went to Pulaski High School, and was familiar with the golf courses, so I would go golfing with him. I didn't do too well, but enjoyed his company. At the end of the first year we were glad to move home for the summer. At the end of the first year, I was ranked about 9th out of 104 students scholastically. I felt pretty good about that as the students came from big universities and small colleges from all over the country, but probably none of them came from small town like Dell Rapids, South Dakota.

During the summer, Mary and I were home with her folks. We stayed with her folks because our house was so crowded with the Aucutt's, the Olin Odland's, plus my mother and dad. During the summer of 1949, I painted the John Hermanson residence. This was sort of a difficult paint job because it's a brick colonial house with shutters and ivory windowpanes and ivory trim. It's a beautiful two-story colonial house, but I always had to watch it so I didn't spill any paint on the bricks. In addition to this, the downstairs windows had 36 panes, and not the kind that you could remove the inserts. These had to be individually painted and it took forever. I guess it's a good thing that I didn't have any other jobs that summer because by the middle of July, Mary and I, and her folks took a nice trip to the Black Hills and then on to Yellowstone. We both enjoyed this trip immensely and then returned from these areas to get lined up for a second year in Milwaukee. By this time my father was 60 years old, and my mother was 58 years old, and they were busy with church work at Dell Rapids Lutheran Church.

The second year of medical school is usually felt to be the hardest year of medical school, at least at that time it was considered to be so. I had to increase my amount of studying. The courses were as follows: Pathology was a yearlong course (both semesters), Physiology was a yearlong course (2 semesters), and in the first semester we had Pharmacology and in the second semester Bacteriology. I believe there were a couple of smaller courses, too, both semesters. But these were the big courses.

Pathology, of course, is the study of diseased tissue microscopically and grossly, and Pharmacology is the study of drugs and their reactions and so forth. Bacteriology was the study of bacteria and viruses. Physiology is the study of the function of the different systems in the body. Our Professor of Physiology was Dr. Percy Swendal, and what a character. He could be very funny, but he just drove everybody nuts with his theories. Dr. Beckman, who wrote a book about Pharmacology, was our Pharmacology professor. Pathology was taught by Dr. W.A.D. Anderson, who also had a big book at that time and was a Professor of Pathology. We had several other pathology professors, of course, in laboratory and lecture periods.

In pathology lab I sat by Paul Oudenhoven on one side, and on the other side was the Norman brothers, Mark and Paul. Actually, I think they were cousins. We were put in alphabetical order for our pathology lab in which we spent day after day looking at slides and gross specimens. We also attended autopsies. Everyone worried, of course, day in and day out about passing different courses because a few did not return after the first year. One of the saddest cases was Antone (Tony) Barrette. Tony didn't pass the first year so he had to take the whole year over and he felt so bad because he didn't have the money, but he did slave through it and with his wife working and everything he did make it through medical school a year after the rest of us who graduated in '52.

Of course, we made the trip home at Christmas, like usual, and had the usual family celebrations. We returned to Milwaukee the second semester and pretty much the same schedule of studying was undertaken. By now, Mary had a different job. She was working for Glauwe's Water Softening Company across the street from our apartment, which was certainly much more convenient. I'm not sure what she was doing, but she claims that she was testing water for softening and so forth. In the meantime, she had met a lady at the office who in the future became good friends with us. Their names were Bob and Katherine Ridel. This, of course, was 1950. In the spring of 1950, about May 1st, we had the good news that Mary was pregnant. We were getting used to our smaller apartment on State Street (7605 West State Street in Wauwatosa) but we had to start thinking for the future when the baby would come, that we would have to possibly get a larger apartment.

I did finish the second year and my ranking in the class had gone to #5. I still felt real good about this, and we were getting accustomed to the fact that possibly we might get through medical school together. I say "together" because this was an experience for the wife, too. We decided mutually that we would stay in Milwaukee during the summer of 1950, and I would extern at St. Joseph's Hospital in Milwaukee. An extern is an undergraduate medical school student who wears a white coat around and helps draw blood and helps the doctors with menial tasks such as doing histories and physicals on people. Also, you do get paid for it.

St. Joseph's Hospital is in the north part of Milwaukee and is a private Catholic hospital of about 600 beds. The externship was very beneficial and we enjoyed our summer in Milwaukee, although we did get away to Dell Rapids and back just before the summer started. The trip to Milwaukee from Dell Rapids is approximately 535 miles by the old Highway 16, which went all the way from Sioux Falls to Milwaukee, through the Wisconsin towns of Madison and Lacrosse.

When the third year of medical school came, the courses

advanced quite rapidly. The basic courses were Internal Medicine and General Surgery, Advanced Pharmacology, Pathologic Physiology, Ophthalmology, Ear, Nose, & Throat, Neurology, Neurosurgery, Gynecology, and Obstetrics, to name a few. I think there were approximately 12 courses during the year. It made it very difficult to keep up with all of these courses with so much reading and attending clinics. By then we were attending clinics in Milwaukee County Emergency Hospital and the beautiful, 1,000 bed Milwaukee County Hospital.

Of course, the pregnancy was progressing. Mary was seeing a Dr. Paul Lee, and uncle of Jack Brown, who was my medical school classmate. Dr. Lee had an office in his house on the north side of Milwaukee. I would take Mary up there for her visits and then I would wait there for her to get through with her checkup. Dr. Lee at that time was probably in his 60's and quite an easygoing person with no major obstetric staff privileges at St. Joseph Hospital, as we found out later. Mary had a very difficult labor, and the baby was a posterior and they had to call in a Dr. Darling, an obstetrician, to use mid-forceps and rotate the baby's head. It turned out to be at least 16 hours of hard labor.

Our son, Donald Mark Odland Jr., as we named him, was born at St. Joseph's Hospital on October 26th, 1950. He weighed 8 lbs. 6 oz. After about 4 days of postpartum care, Mary was allowed to come home and her mother came to stay with us for a while. The total bill for the hospital was $85.00, and the obstetrical doctor bill was canceled because I was a medical student. Of course, little Mark took a lot of our time from then on, in addition to my schoolwork. Mary went full time as a mother and had to quit her job with Glauwe Water Softening Company. We were fast finding that the one bedroom apartment was pretty cramped.

Christmas 1950. We made the trip home to Dell Rapids with little Mark, which we called him instead of getting mixed up with Donald Mark Jr. The trip home was rather uneventful. We made the trip back in real bad weather. We started out with a 6-week old baby and we got halfway across Minnesota going east, and it started snowing. By the time we got to Lacrosse, we could hardly see the road anymore. I had to get back so we made the excuse that we had to get back and continued on our way. We reached Madison, Wisconsin, and then the roads turned to ice. This is probably the worst trip we have ever made at any time as a family.

It was raining, and the rain was coming from Lake Michigan. It was freezing on our windshield so I had to get out every 3-4 miles and chip off ice. In the meantime, the highway became real slippery, and I tried to drive on the edge of the road. It was so slippery I was afraid to turn off to a farmyard any place. We finally go to an area west of Milwaukee and there was a big hill. Semis were jackknifed all over the place. I was able to wind my way through the semis and finally go to our apartment. The ice on the car was probably close to an inch thick. We thanked God that we made it in this time. Everybody at home was worried about us.

In the meantime, we did get another apartment. This apartment was in a new apartment house on 8920 West Blue Mound Avenue. This was really nice. We had a parking lot in back, a back door on the first floor, and a front door. We had a larger living room, a separate kitchen and a little dining room off the kitchen, and a larger bedroom. Our neighbors across the hallway were Bob and Katherine Ridel. Upstairs were Joe and Ed (I forget the name of the other couple above Ridel's). There were 8 apartments in each building, and there were 2 buildings. Everybody got along real well and it was a very pleasant place to live.

I forgot to mention that when going home for Christmas, Mary went ahead on the train and then we came back together in the car. Her folks were able to meet her in

Brookings, South Dakota. Then I finished out the junior year of medical school and was ranked 3rd in the class. I believe we went home that summer and I worked at Morrell's to pick up some extra money. In the evenings, I would spend time at the house with my folks off and on. We would sit out on the sun porch and talk about old times together with other relatives. I remember that my father just loved Root Beer and Root Beer floats. He would either make homemade Root Beer or buy Root Beer by the gallon and then have vanilla ice cream, making Root Beer floats. He loved to talk about old times. A lot of times he would be silent. We would be talking most of the time and sometimes he would chide in a little.

Then back to Milwaukee in September of 1951, our last year of medical school. By now, little Mark was approaching 1 year of age. During the senior year, there would be more clinics plus a lot of studying. By now, we were taking a lot of movies of Mark as he was growing. Also, Mark was "adopted" by our neighbors across the hall, Bob and Catherine. They doted on him. We made a couple of trips out to Waterford, Wisconsin, which is the home of Catherine's mother. With Jo, Ed, Bob, Catherine, and ourselves and Mark, we would go to this place and have picnics. Neither of these couples had any children and actually didn't have any in the future either, so they were very interested in the growth of Mark.

It's hard to remember exactly where I had these different 3-month periods, but we had 3, 3-month sections, in which we concentrated on one particular subject. For instance, I had internal medicine at Milwaukee County Hospital for 3 months. That meant classes, rounds, diagnosis, history, and physicals on patients there. Then I had 3 months at St. Joseph's Hospital in obstetrics and gynecology. This was very interesting. The first 24 hours I was there on obstetrics, we had close to 24 babies. For the month I was there (the first month) we had 375 babies. They had 8 delivery rooms and a big black board on which they kept track of the progress of the labors of these different women. It reminded me of a race where one was racing the other. This was a very valuable time to learn a lot about obstetrics and forceps deliveries, and I was able to do a lot of deliveries, and a lot of episiotomies, and so forth. Dr. Jack Kliger was the doctor in charge of obstetrics.

Then I spent 3 months at Wood Veterans Hospital. This was on the surgical rotation and we scrubbed every day in surgery for at least 4-6 hours per day, plus rounds, and it became very long and we had to stay overnight quite a few times. My main mentor was Dr. Beno, and I was warned ahead of time about him. He was a young surgeon, but he was very particular and taught me many things about surgery. I would scrub in with him every day. Also, we had about 3-4 weeks on chest surgery. These cases were mostly lung tumors and tuberculosis cases. At that time, tuberculosis patients were isolated and everybody wore yellow scrubs, and the patients also wore yellow to distinguish them from other people. This consisted mostly of lung resections where they would give a person drugs, like Isoniazid, and then follow it with surgery to remove diseased parts of the lungs. These were extensively long cases on very debilitated persons.

CHAPTER 8

DR. DON

Indeed, the body does not consist of one member but of many. If the foot would say, "Because I am not a hand, I do not belong to the body," that would not make it any less a part of the body. And if the ear would say, "Because I am not an eye, I do not belong to the body," that would not make it any less a part of the body. If the whole body were an eye, where would the hearing be? If the whole body were hearing, where would the sense of smell be? But as it is, God arranged the members in the body, each one of them, as he chose. If all were a single member, where would the body be? As it is, there are many members, yet one body.

(1 Corinthians 12:14-20)

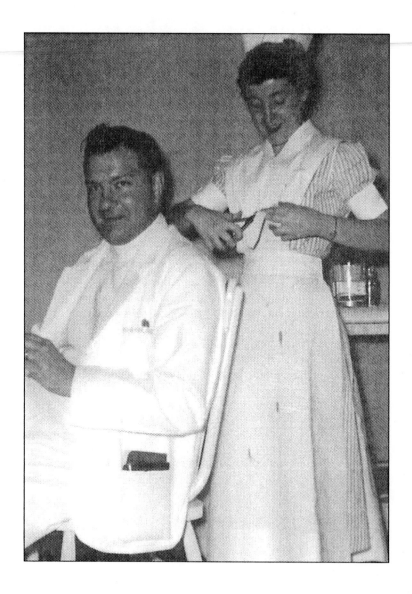

Then came the spring of 1952. We had to make our choices for the following summer, as to where we would go for internships. My first choice was Minneapolis General Hospital, to get closer to home. My second choice was St. Joseph's Hospital, and the third choice was Milwaukee County Hospital. I did receive my first choice, which was Minneapolis General Hospital, Minneapolis, Minnesota. Then graduation came. John and Alice Hermanson (my in-laws), my father, Ole Odland, and my mother Clara Odland all came out. Also, my brother Paul and Barbara were there.

Graduation was held in conjunction with the undergraduates, the nursing students, the law students, and engineering students at Milwaukee Auditorium. There were close to 1,500 graduates. There were about 90 medical students that graduated out of a class of 104 that started. It was a very impressive graduation in which you got your Doctor's degree as well as a Doctor's gown with the Doctor of Medicine stole wrapped around your collar. Of course, we realized that we would probably never see most of these fellows again. But I gave special attention to the fact that I would keep in contact with a few of them.

My close friend by now, Ben Strehlow, was one of these people. As I mentioned before, his wife, Katherine, had a mastectomy during the freshman year, and during the sophomore year of medical school, she died, after having a baby named Charles Strehlow. During the sophomore year, Ben had to get up real early and take care of the baby and his wife, and finally she died and he had to hire a babysitter. He made it all the way through medical school. Ben stayed on at Milwaukee County Hospital as an intern. Jack Brown stayed on as an intern at St. Joseph's Hospital.

Others spread out all over the country. Several of the New York boys went back to New York hospitals while Walt Parmley went to California. He already had his law degree before he started medical school, but then he went on into ophthalmology. I really never heard from him again. Anyhow, we graduated and took pictures, etc. Then after graduation we decided to drive all night to get home. We had packed before we started. There was a caravan of 3 cars, the Ole Odland's, John Hermanson's, and Donald Odland's. As we got to the Lacrosse area, we hit a terrible rainstorm, but we weathered through it. Now I was driving a 1950 Dodge, which my father-in-law had given us.

On April 13, prior to graduation, we had a big car accident with this 1950 Dodge. We were driving south on Easter Sunday morning towards Evanston, where we were going to meet with Mary's uncle, Maurice, and his wife and family, and have Easter dinner with them. We had been there before. We got to an intersection just north of Waukegan, Illinois, and as I pulled into the intersection the person in front of me stopped real suddenly on a yellow light and I crashed into the back of their car! In the process, I slid sideways and practically demolished my driver's side of the car. Little Mark was in a car seat, but the car seats were so flimsy at that time, the car seat was really bent to an unusable state, but he was okay. None of us really got hurt.

We had to take the train back and have the car towed back to Milwaukee. Somehow I had to get this car back to

166

Dell Rapids to have it repaired. Mary went ahead for Easter (this is all prior to graduation, I'm backtracking a little now!) on the train. She was met by her folks at Brookings. They took her to Dell Rapids with little Mark. I drove home at Easter with the left side (about 1/3 of the car) smashed in, so that if it rained I would get very wet because it was like a convertible top. About 1/3 of the roof was pushed in over the driver's side. The driver's door had to be tied in place. There were floods at that time also, but I was able to drive home safely. We were able to borrow another car to get through the rest of the school year.

When we got home after graduation there was very little time before starting internship on July 1, 1952, at Minneapolis General Hospital in Minneapolis, Minnesota. In the meantime, I remember my mother and dad had their 35th wedding anniversary in June of 1952. We had a reunion of the Odland side in Dell Rapids, as well as some of the Stenslands. I took movies of the gathering at the parsonage in Dell Rapids, and for some reason, have misplaced this movie. The movie, as I remember, is priceless because my father was in good health at that time and several of his brothers arrived for this 35th anniversary. By then, Mark was 1 and ½ years old.

We then proceeded to Minneapolis to find an apartment, and found one on 4605 South Nicollet Avenue. At that time, the area was fairly good, but an older neighborhood. The apartment was on the second floor and was rather dark and not in the best of shape. So, when we left Milwaukee, Mary and I had been very happy as far as our apartment was concerned. But now, all of a sudden, we were in a different community, in a different neighborhood, with a rather backward-looking apartment. The unfortunate part is that Mary had long days alone and long nights alone.

Minneapolis General Hospital at that time was a very old hospital and was owned by the City of Minneapolis. For the most part, the hospital took care of the indigent and less privileged people, but also took care of the emergencies for the city and most of Hennepin County. We did see some private patients also. The hospital had a lot of wards. A ward would be ideal for nurses and doctors, but not so private for patients. I found my rotation would be with Donald Fox, M.D. and Gerald Cady, M.D. To begin with, we had every-third-night duty and they were tough nights. It was an extremely hard working year. We three doctors started out on the neurology service seeing a lot of stroke patients and brain tumors and so forth. We had residents over us, and had consulting doctors over them. It was an old hospital but it taught you humility and hard work, and the experience was a great thing.

A ward might have 30 patients in it with only screens between them, all in one big room. This was great when you were making rounds, but like I said before, very little privacy for the patient. Also, it was great for nursing service because they could view the whole ward at night and spot problems easily. During this year, we rotated from service to service, that is, form neurosurgery to internal medicine and to general surgery, and then spent some time working in the emergency room and riding the ambulance. The ambulances were driven by Minneapolis police officers, and we got to know several of them quite well.

In some cities in the country they had taken the doctors off ambulances. In St. Louis, I remember, they had 2 doctors killed on these runs. These ambulance runs were really quite hair-raising. It was like nothing to be going down Central Avenue going north at 70 mph. I did experience being in an ambulance wreck. We had just picked up a boy who was hurt in north Minneapolis, and his grandmother rode in the back of the ambulance with the boy and me. The two policemen were in the front driving the ambulance. We got going down the road and hit a car driven by some University of

Minnesota students. Nobody was actually hurt but it was quite an experience.

On some services we had to be on duty every-other-night. When we were on duty at night, it was all night that you would be awake. Then you would have to be on duty the next day. Finally, if you were lucky, you would get home the following night at 8:00, and then have to be back at the hospital at 7:00 the next morning and go through the same thing again. This really meant you were on for about 36 hours in a row and off about 8 hours, and then right back on schedule again. This was a very depressing beginning for Mary and Mark in the Nicollet Avenue apartment. When we were on the orthopedic and fracture service, we were able to set a lot of fractures with help from consultants, and were taught a great deal.

Mary's folks, John and Alice, came to Minneapolis to visit us, and the 4 of us decided that it would be best if we could try to get into a different apartment situation. We were very fortunate in getting into the Minnakada Court Apartments. These apartments were on West Excelsior Blvd., just past France Avenue. At first, we had a semi-half level down basement apartment, and later on moved to the first floor. There we met a lot of good friends, among them the Howard Kirst family. Also, there was a family above us and he was an FBI agent and we got to know them pretty well. Little Mark was able to play with Mary Ellen Kirst. They became good friends, riding their trikes up and down the sidewalks. It was a very pleasant place because it was off the main street and down off a hill, and there were no problems as far as keeping track of the kids and so forth. I don't believe we were even able to get back home to Dell Rapids that Christmas because I was on duty all the time.

When I was on the obstetrical service, I suddenly had an attack of appendicitis and thereby had to have an operation. One of the staff doctors did the operation and a couple of my buddies assisted, and I can remember going to sleep and they looked down at me and said, "We get this one." At that time, they would give you shots around the clock for antibiotics, just routinely. The shot was Pen-Strep, a combination of Penicillin and Streptomycin, which, looking back was sort of a poor excuse for treatment. But that's the way it was done then. The reason I bring this up is later on, about 6 weeks later, I took some penicillin orally and had a reaction so that I had to miss work for a while because they thought I had rheumatic fever, but it was a penicillin reaction. So, from then on I was considered allergic to penicillin.

In the spring of 1953, David Odland was born, and his name would be David John Odland, born on March 19, 1953. The baby was born at Minneapolis General Hospital, and I was on duty in the ER when they called me up and said, "Your wife has just had a baby boy" and I was allowed to go up and see her (wasn't that nice?). She did have a private room but was surrounded by a lot of minority mothers and unwed mothers, and in those days that was quite a different kind of situation, and probably much more common nowadays. But she got along fine and had a good postpartum course. She was able to go home with little David. Her mother came to stay with us for a little while, and it's sure a good thing we moved to a different apartment, which had 2 bedrooms.

Towards the end of that first year of internship, we had to make a decision as to what to do as far as the future was concerned. I decided that the thing I really liked about medicine was general surgery, so I applied for a residency in this particular field and was accepted at Minneapolis General Hospital for one of the four slots for general surgery residency. One of the other residents or interns chosen for that was Dr. Schafhausen. This residency started on July 1st 1953. So, of course, we stayed on at the same apartment location. During your internship at Minneapolis

General, you would wear intern's uniforms, that is, white shoes, white trousers, and white short zippered-up type of white tops with your name written under your left pocket in red. You were given several of these.

The pay that we had during internship was $50.00 a month (close to $0.18/hour, figuring a 75-hour week). During the internship, there was a continuing and worsening epidemic of polio. This, of course, was before oral and injectable polio vaccine. During the year that I was at General Hospital for internship, we had over 900 cases of polio and over 120 deaths from bulbar polio. One of the areas of the hospital was devoted entirely to polio patients. It was a frightening experience and a frightening disease. I remember distinctly, one young fellow coming to the desk at the emergency room and stating, "I don't feel so good, I think I have a fever, and I can't swallow very well," and by the time we got him over to the other unit where they take care of polio patients, he only lasted 4 hours and died of bulbar polio. People nowadays don't realize how bad it was. They also don't realize how wonderful these vaccines have been.

July 1st 1953. At the end of the rotating internship at Minneapolis General Hospital, I started my surgical residency as a first year resident. I had already been exposed to a lot of surgery during my senior year of medical school and my year of internship. I had a good friend, Dick Lindquist, who was at Mayo Clinic taking surgery residency, and the first 2 years of their surgical residency they didn't get to do any operating, even under supervision. When I went down to see him once he was carrying surgical specimens to the pathology lab and spending 6 months there, which all was part of the surgical residency, of course.

I'm sure that was very good training, but for me, I wanted to get into the more practical operative part of the surgical residency, and lo and behold, it wasn't long before I was right into the thick of it. We had 6 operating rooms on the top floor in what was known as the surgical suite. At that time, it was not air-conditioned, and it was pretty hot sometimes at night. We finally invited the city council members down to see how hot it would get in the operating rooms and put gowns and everything on them, and it was about 94 degrees in the operating room. It wasn't too long before we had air-conditioning. This helped considerably.

We had very good supervision with some excellent surgeons supervising our care, and we also assisted them. I'll never forget Dr. E. P. Eder, who was a whiz at general surgery. Also, there was Malcolm McCannel, who actually was a senior resident. Then there was Dr. Nelson, also a senior resident, and Dr. Holian. These senior residents were very good in their 4th year of surgery. They were great teachers and I assisted them on major procedures. It wasn't long before I was involved with my own operations as well. I remember one of the first days in general surgery Dr. Eder scheduled me to help him with a vein operation. It was a bilateral saphenous vein stripping. Just as we were making incisions, he left the room and said, "I'll be back later," leaving me, some nurse assistants, and an intern to help. This turned out to be a rather tough case, but he would step in every once in a while and give me some help and assistance, and then leave again. This way, you were baptized into the field of general surgery.

We had surgical rounds every day (morning and evening) on surgical patients (there were about 30 of them) in the surgical ward. It was an open ward, as I described before. In addition to this, we had a lot of surgery night and day. Another doctor and I were on every other night, and it certainly left Mary alone a lot. I would have to be at the operating room by 6:30, scrub in for surgery about 7:00-7:30, and then go until 2:00-3:00 in the afternoon. We would sometimes take emergency room call and stay all night, the next day, and finally leave the hospital around

5:00 at night. One time I was so tired I just fell asleep in the doctor's lounge. Somebody came and woke me up at 8:00 in the evening and said, "Your wife called to see if you weren't coming home." Of course, then you get home and you're tired and have a late supper and go to bed, and get up again and start the whole thing over. This went on for a solid year. The only break in this kind of a schedule was when I was on emergency room and was in charge of the Minneapolis General Hospital ER for 2 months.

At that time, I would be in charge of the interns and under the supervision of consultants, and would actually help run the ER for everybody. I would see about 150 patients a day coming through the emergency room setting. I didn't have to see all the patients, but I would see the more interesting patients and over-read all the x-rays for the ER patients. This was some kind of crazy schedule. I can hardly repeat it! It was something like 24 on and 12 off, then 24 on again, or something like that. This went on for 6-8 weeks. Then somebody else would rotate through the system.

We had a lot of trauma cases come in, including bullet wounds, stab wounds, and shotgun wounds. In fact, I got so I was really able to handle bullet and shotgun wounds, knifings, and stab wounds. While you are in the ER, you would see a lot of acute abdominal cases, which you would refer upstairs and make a diagnosis to go to surgery and so forth, and then follow it up with operating room cases upstairs. In this manner, I got a lot of experience. We continued to get paid about $150.00 a month, but in addition to that, we're paid extra by the city for emergency room care. The pay, of course, was nothing like it is nowadays. I think we were paid $75.00 extra for 24 hours of emergency room care.

In general surgery, I was exposed to and did a lot of procedures, including varicose veins, hemorrhoidectomies, gallbladders (cholecystectomies), and subtotal gastrectomies, as well as total gastrectomies, splenectomies, appendectomies, and bowel resections. Most of these procedures, even within 6 months, we were doing ourselves. I kept a complete record and log of everything I did. I was involved with ENT service and radical necks and laryngectomies. Part of our service also was fracture care. We had a lot of fractured hips and fractured tibias and femurs, motorcycle accidents, and so forth. In fact, we worked (pardon the expression) damn hard. I remember one particular 24-hour period when we were in the operating room 22 out of 24 hours with hardly any breaks. We would maybe grab a quick sandwich in between cases. This was when we had an onslaught of surgical trauma cases coming in from car accidents. Of course, knowing the Twin City area, it was the belt line, and the accidents were terrible. Since then, of course, they have built another ring around the Cities.

I was also involved in some research in blood volume studies with "Evans Blue" testing, which we thought was pretty good, but later on was replaced by other methods. Then I was able to go to the Vet's Hospital for part of my rotation (about 2 months). At that time, we did a lot of coronary heart surgery and lung resections on chest surgery. I became very involved in chest surgery. In fact, I did a few small wedge resections myself with one of the other residents assisting. There is a Dr. Brown out there at the Vet's Hospital, who was a senior resident, and also Dr. G. The consultants were Dr. Schmidt (I forget his first name) and another doctor.

Dr. G tried to talk me into going into chest surgery, but I made some observations while there. He was really fun to work with and an excellent surgeon and he was involved in the early workings of coronary heart surgery. He showed me his dog lab where he would narrow the coronary arteries by clamps (he had a system for doing that) and was able to try and produce coronary artery stenosis. He would then do some procedures by tunneling the internal mammary artery under the coronary artery and try to provide more capillary circulation through the connections under the muscle of the myocardium. This was an experimental procedure, and seemed to work pretty well, but, of course, progress led to greater things in the future. I often thought if I had taken that route that I would have been a pioneer in coronary surgery, but I did not make that choice.

One thing that bothered me was that we spent an awful lot of time at the Vet's Hospital. I was away from home a lot and Dr. Brown and Dr. G were already divorced because their wives couldn't stand their absence, and I talked to them about that and they said, well, this was one sacrifice they had to make. I was not willing at that time to leave the family alone and shirk my responsibility completely, so I didn't continue on that particular course. We found time to take the two young boys to different things, especially in the warm weather to the Lake Calhoun and Lake Harriet beaches and have picnics and so forth. And, of course, we made some trips home, although we were really tied down by my schedule.

In the spring of 1954, we had quite a shock because we went home about Easter time and people in the Dell Rapids congregation stopped us after church and said, "Do you notice anything wrong with your dad?" We said, "No, we hadn't noticed anything special." Several people came up to us and said, "You've got to do something about your dad, he's having some spells in the pulpit." Apparently he would stop and sort of stare right in the middle of the sermon, maybe just for 5 seconds, but you count out 5 seconds in front of an audience and that was quite a problem. By brothers and I finally convinced him to go to Minneapolis, to the University of Minnesota Hospital and have a complete checkup by the world famous neurologist, Dr. Baker. At that time, my father was 64 years of age.

Dr. Baker came out after the examination and said, "Your father has Lou Gehrig Disease," which is also amyotrophic lateral sclerosis. He also said he had the bulbar type (that's the cranial nerve type and upper cervical and thoracic nerve type) that will cause him to be dead in about a year. Well, this was very difficult to accept because he looked so young and healthy for his age. He hardly had a gray hair on his head. He had also always been very muscular and active and full of enthusiasm, especially for his work in the ministry. Well, things did progress, as I'll discuss later.

For several reasons, I decided by then that maybe I should try to move to a location and get started in the practice of medicine, most likely general practice and surgery. I hoped to practice in a town anywhere from 4,000-10,000. Also, I was getting tired of depending on my father-in-law for money to help us get through these difficult years. I was approximately 27 and ½ years of age. By this time (that is, in the spring of 1954), Mark was 3 and ½ years old, and David was 1 year old. So, I would spend my weekends looking.

I went to Ortonville, Minnesota, and talked to a doctor out there, but I wasn't too impressed with the set-up, so then I went to Waseca and talked to a Dr. Swenson there, as I knew his son who was an intern with me. But, it didn't look too likely that I wanted to locate there, although I liked the town. I also went down to Albert Lea, talked to a Dr. Palmer there (I'm sure he's dead by now). He invited me to his home, which was a huge home on Fountain Lake in Albert Lea. He brought a couple of older doctors over to see me and there were 3 of them, and they were excited to have me possibly join them and practice medicine. I did notice that they kept talking about retirement and it would be only me and another young fellow who would possibly be paying them off so they could retire. I will always second-guess myself as to whether or not I should've gone on into full general surgery residency and also possibly into chest surgery and heart surgery, but then that's water over the dam.

Then my brother-in-law, Dr. John Hermanson, from Valley Springs, South Dakota, wanted me to come down and look at Luverne, Minnesota, as he stated that there was a shortage of doctors in Luverne. So, Mary and I went to Dell Rapids to visit the folks, and left the kids over there, and together with John Hermanson, Sr., went to Luverne to look at prospects there. I first parked at the Rock County Bank corner and I went across the street, and Dr. Bofenkamp at that time was the doctor over the First National Bank, which is now the City Hall. He was upstairs and I went up to see him. It was very discouraging because he just told me, "Why don't you go back to Minneapolis and finish your specialty, and then go someplace other than Luverne, because we don't really need you here."

Then I went down the street where Piggly-Wiggly store was and Dr. Sherman was upstairs. Dr. Charles L. Sherman had already been in Luverne 50-some years, and I went in to talk to him, and he was very congenial but he also stated, "I think the future would be for you to specialize in surgery and stay in the Cities" or something like that. "I really don't see any future for you here in Luverne. We're all as busy as we want to be but we really don't need another doctor." I went up to the hospital and looked around and, oh my gosh, a 2-story hospital built in 1915, and very antiquated. I'll discuss this later when I did actually move to Luverne.

Well, I was ready to go back to Dell Rapids and forget about Luverne, but then Mary said, "Why don't we go and see the other younger doctors?" So I went over and talked to Dr. Ervin Boone, and at that time he was located in an office, which is now a 2nd hand store on McKenzie, just south of Main Street. I talked to Dr. Boone and he said, "Oh, we sure need help. I'm so busy I can hardly take it." He showed me around a little, was very congenial, and stated that there was a possibility that they were trying to draft doctors, and if I moved into town they might have a problem with that, but he still encouraged me to come to Luverne.

Then I went to see Dr. Albert C. Martin, and he was

located on Cedar Street, just north of the Rock County bank corner. Again, this conversation was very good. He was very busy, and he stated that he would be more than willing to welcome me to the city of Luverne because they needed help. Then I had some talks with my father-in-law, my wife, and Dr. John, my brother-in-law in Valley Springs, and decided that Luverne would be the place to come if we could find housing and find perspective office space.

We went back to the Cities and tried to discuss this more, and decide whether or not Luverne would be a good town to go to. There were some other extenuating circumstances, such as my father's illness. The question came up whether he had 1 year to live or not. Would I feel satisfied working my tail off in Minneapolis in a residency and knowing that I wouldn't see my dad but once or twice more before he died? So, this did become part of the decision, although a lot of people told me to forget that kind of an attitude towards it. But it bothered me so much that I had to consider it. At that time, I felt I could start in Luverne and always move on some place later on. Then we did make the decision to go to Luverne. There were some preparations to make, such as finding office space and finding a home.

During the last 2 months of my residency the consulting doctors and senior residents all knew I was going to be leaving, so they would feed me cases like everything, especially things like fractured hips and fractured tibias, trauma work, gallbladder operations, appendectomies, vein operations, and so forth. Also, they would set up cases like cystoceles, rectoceles, hysterectomies, and other cases, and I put in a lot of time doing surgery. They knew that I would be pressed to do a lot of these things in a small town so they tried to prepare me as best they could. In the meantime, they had several conferences with me and tried to talk me out of leaving the residency at the end of the first year.

CHAPTER 9

A NEW LIFE IN LUVERNE

"Everyone then who hears these words of mine and acts on them will be like a wise man who built his house on rock. The rain fell, the floods came, and the winds blew and beat on that house, but it did not fall, because it had been founded on rock. And everyone who hears these words of mine and does not act on them will be like a foolish man who built his house on sand. The rain fell, and the floods came, and the winds blew and beat against that house, and it fell - and great was its fall!"

(Matthew 7:24-27)

W e made a couple more trips to Luverne and picked out some office space over the Pat's Plumbing building, owned by W.L Krug. As you went up the stairway between Piggly-Wiggly store and Pat's Plumbing (it was a rather wide stairway with 22 steps to the top, which was a stress test for anybody), a right turn at the top of the stairs took you to Dr. Sherman's office. If you turned left, you went to my office. I had rented 3 rooms, which were sort of attractive. One was a long room, which was the waiting room, but the dark room was right off the waiting room, which was an inconvenience. There were two offices. One was more or less a consulting type of office with my desk and so forth, and the other room was rather large, facing the street, with windows on Main Street, looking south. They had Venetian blinds. One room was sort of a minor surgery and examining room. Across the hall was an x-ray room, and down the hall was a pathology room. I had to buy a lot of equipment.

We looked around town with Marion Frakes at that time and bought a house on West Brown Street, on the south side. The address was 419 West Brown Street. It was a 2-story Cape Cod type, and it's still there. Now, this particular house had 5 bedrooms, 2 down and 3 up, all rather small but adequate. We didn't need 5 bedrooms. We made 1 bedroom on the southwest part of the first floor into a den and the one on the northwest was a guest bedroom. We and the 2 boys slept upstairs. This house was previously owned by Marion Frakes and his wife, and they had lived there and they also built the house. We bought it for $20,500, with some assistance from John Hermanson, Sr., on the initial down payment. This location had a big back lot with some fairly good sized trees, and had a single car garage and a full basement. It had a little L-shaped living room and dining room, and a kitchen with a little area for a table and chairs. We pretty much brought all of our furniture with us from Minneapolis.

At this point, I'll describe some of the medical facilities in town at that time. First of all, there were 4 doctors, all separate in their practices. Nobody combined. No dual practices or partnerships existed at that time. There was Charles L. Sherman, M.D., and F.W. Bofenkamp (Ferdinand), M.D. I would estimate Dr. Sherman's age at that time to be approximately 80 years of age. I also would estimate Dr. Bofenkamp's age at about 55 years of age. Albert C. Martin, M.D. and Ervin S. Boone were the 2 younger doctors. Dr. Boone was around 30 years of age and Dr. Martin probably was about 32 years of age.

Regarding the hospital facilities in Luverne at that time, the block was encompassed by McKenzie Street on the west and Spring Street on the east, Brown Street on the north and Luverne Street on the south. This was the so-called hospital block as it now is located. At that time, there were houses on the east side of the block and on the north side, and there was a house on the corner called the nurse's residence, which, at the time I came to Luverne, was occupied by Dale Garris and his wife. Dale was the administrator of the Luverne Community Hospital. At that time it was called Luverne City Hospital. On the southwest corner of the block was located Our Savior's Lutheran Church.

Just across from the sheriff's office, on the west side of

the street on McKenzie, was the city hospital. This old city hospital, and I mean old, was just south of the nurse's residence, or the administrator's residence as it was at that time. The hospital was constructed, as I recall, in about 1910, and was typical of some of the older small town hospitals. You would enter from the west side and there were about 6 or 8 steps up to the front porch, which is all concrete and brick enclosed, and you would come right in the main hallway. There would be a double patient room on the left side as you walked in the door into the hallway, and also a 4-place room on the right side. Then you would walk a little further down the hallway and you would walk to the right, and there was a dining room and kitchen behind it, and a small office for the administrator. Back by the kitchen was a small laboratory, very small. Then to the left, past the first room on the left side, there was a stairway (quite large) going up to the second floor.

Also, at that place, there was a stairway going down to the basement with an entrance to the side, so that the administrator could get in and out of the hospital quite easily. This entrance was on the north side. Then there was an elevator right next to the stairway that would take you to the basement, 1st floor, and 2nd floor. This was not an electric elevator. This was a rope drawn elevator such a I had seen when I worked at a grocery store several years before to help carry freight up and down (I'll comment on the elevator later). Then just east of that would be another patient's room and another patient's room east of that, and then a back entrance on the east side. Later on, about 1 and ½-2 years later, Dr. Rohrer came to be our radiologist and we did buy an x-ray machine at that time. But when I came to Luverne, we had only a portable x-ray machine. Going up the stairs to the 2nd floor, there was a patient's room over the porch and a patient's room on the northwest and southwest corners.

Then, of course, was the upstairs elevator entrance. On

the northeast corner was the operating room and sterilization room. The operating room had windows so if you were real hungry you could open a window and pick apples off the apple tree. On the southeast corner of the hospital was the delivery room and labor room, all combined. Then there was a postpartum room in the middle that housed usually 3 or 4 patients. There was also a nursery off the hallway on the east side. Actually, this nursery seemed to be more or less a closet. It was probably 10-15 ft. long and 6 ft. wide with some bassinets in the area. The hospital wasn't air-conditioned and sometimes in the summer it got very warm, especially in the nursery. One time I was called over and a baby had a 106 fever, and it was mainly because it was 104 outside. We had to take the baby into another room and cool the baby off, and the baby was alright with no sickness involved. If it got real hot in the labor and delivery room, we would have to open the windows, but you can imagine what happened in the summertime when you open the windows with little gnats flying in and out. I'm not trying to degrade the hospital, but this is the way it was.

I really felt like I had arrived at a mission hospital. Considering the fact that I did work at Minneapolis General Hospital, which was rather antiquated at the time, that wasn't such a big change, but coming from the Vet's Hospital in Minneapolis, which was brand new, was quite a change. Then I looked over the surgical instruments and we had quite a problem there. The abdominal surgery instruments were very inadequate. There were no vein stripping instruments, so one of the first things I had to do was sit down and go over all of these instruments and try to figure out what we really needed to progress to a more modern era. Also, each of the doctors had their own instrument packs for different things like appendectomies and tonsillectomies, and so here I was without any instruments to really call my own or work with. They were, however, very gracious and let me use their instruments.

The charge nurse at that time was Mrs. C. H. (I'm going to use initials from now on). There also was Mrs. T. B. and many other excellent nurses on the staff. Mr. Dale Garris was the administrator and his wife was a nurse anesthetist. Also, at times, all of the doctors gave anesthesia for the other doctors. Although I had had some training in anesthesia, I felt very inadequate at this particular point, doing this type of procedure. Shortly after I arrived, I called Dorothy Lamberty, who was my surgical nurse at the Veteran's Hospital at Fort Snelling in Minneapolis. I called her and talked to her about the possibility sometime of her coming down and looking over the situation and seeing if she would be willing to consider in the future, at some time, being the administrator at the Luverne City Hospital. She was originally from Dell Rapids and had connections and family there, so this wasn't completely out of line.

Well, the great adventure was beginning. We had moved into our house and were neatly settled there. We invited Dr. Martin and his wife over to have an evening together and talk things over. I told him at that time that probably I wouldn't see any bullet wounds or knife wounds very much anymore, but that was one thing I was trained in. The reason I bring this up is, the next morning at approximately 8:00, he called me, out of breath and almost panicking, and stated that he had a bullet wound for me. I rushed over to the hospital (this was around the middle of July 1954) and lo and behold, when I got there, there was a female patient. She had been very depressed and had attempted to take her own life by shooting herself with a 22-rifle.

She was the hospital administrator's wife, and was in postpartum depression. All of a sudden, we were faced with a big emergency and found out that we were very short of a lot of equipment. She had a hemopneumothorax on the left side and was in shock. The bullet had perforated through the lung, but just barely missed the heart. We took some portable x-rays and immediately I put in chest tubes to get rid of the hemopneumothorax and re-expand her lung on the left side. We had to make do with a homemade type of chest suction unit, using 3-bottle suction unit. We gathered 3 bottles and were able to put the left chest under negative pressure. We started some oxygen and started IV's, and she started to get better and she did survive.

At that time, the hospital board was made up of, I believe, 5 members, and through this emergency situation with the hospital administrator's own wife, we found that hospital supplies had been dwindling markedly and the hospital was in somewhat of a crisis. I believe, in retrospect, in an effort to make the positive side of the ledger look good, the inventories were allowed to decrease and we could hardly find the right syringes to use for different things. It was shortly after her recovery that the hospital administrator applied for a job in Platte, South Dakota, and moved there.

In defense of Dale, he was caught between a rock and a hard place in trying to administrate a hospital that really had very little financial backing from the community. In an effort to do this, he was trying to keep his job and keep everybody happy. At this time, also, we had a very conservative hospital board. Looking back into the history of the hospital, it was constructed by Dr. Sherman and then later on was sold to the city of Luverne. When I came here, a lot of medical cases went to Mayo Clinic and Sioux Falls, and not too many people really stayed in Luverne. The doctors all realized that we had to promote our hospital more to try and get the community to support it.

Also, there was a building committee, and they were starting to assemble funds by pledges to build a new hospital. When my 2 brother doctors looked at the hospital, they said, "Don, what have you gotten yourself into?" There were times after I came here that I wondered, too, about that. But at that time I felt in a pioneering spirit, and we just did the best we could and moved ahead. Shortly after Dale G. left as administrator, the hospital board hired Dorothy Lamberty to come from Minneapolis to be the administrator, and also head nurse. Then we really went to work, because here was an experienced surgical nurse from a big hospital, and she knew what we needed. I sat down with her, and we ordered a lot of instruments, but nothing compared to nowadays. As a result of acquiring the proper instruments, I was able to start doing more and more general surgery.

One night I had a patient come in, about 50 years old, with a red-hot gallbladder and an acute gangrenous cholecystitus. Dr. Hermanson, my brother-in-law, came from Valley Springs, and we operated on the patient and he did real well. The reason I bring this up is because after the operation we had to load the patient on the elevator on the 2nd floor, and Dr. Hermanson and I went down with the patient and the nurse to the first floor to a patient room. After we got off the elevator, Dr. Hermanson said, "You know, the elevator is more of a risk than the surgery."

If you don't understand what a rope elevator is, they are a system of ropes and pulleys and counter-balances, and there are 2 large ropes that just barely fit in your hand. You would grab a hold of those (ropes) and go up and down and, of course, it's easier to go down than up. There is a break rope, too, that you can pull on one side where it releases and the other side locks. Going down with Dr. Hermanson, the nurse, and me and the patient on a cart, we went down pretty fast, and you can almost get rope burns from it.

That first year in Luverne involved a lot of "firsts." As far as I know I did the first gastric resection in Luverne, Minnesota, in the hospital. Also, I did the first vein stripping. I'm not sure if anybody did any bowel resections in Luverne before, but I did several of those. We had no so-called emergency room, so as a result we had to go on a lot of house calls. If there were any lacerations, they would have to bring the patient to the office so we could repair them there, or sometimes in the hospital surgical area. One of the older doctors talked to Ms. Lamberty and asked her what those instruments were for and she said they were for vein stripping and he said, "Well, how do you use them?" She told me about it and she said she wasn't about to tell him how to use them because she was afraid he might use them. So, here we were, with an x-ray machine in my office, which was rather antiquated, but all I could afford, and the local hospital had only a portable x-ray, which was really a poor excuse.

We had no call system so everybody was on every night. The patients in the community would play one doctor against the other and maybe call you at midnight and if you were tired and couldn't see that it was a real emergency, you say to the patient over the phone, "Well, I'll see you in the morning," and they would say, "Well, I'll call the other doctor then." Well, when you're trying to build a practice from scratch it became important that you would take as many house calls as you could. During that first fall I would probably see 6-9 home calls in the evening. This is in addition to surgery in the morning and seeing patients all day. In fact, sometimes the days ran together with the nights so you didn't know when you would ever get any rest. There was no time off unless you just took it.

After we got settled in our house and started the practice of medicine on July 15, 1954, I saw my first patient at the office. I'm not sure I can recollect how many people I saw that first day, possibly 4 or 5. There are always some people who want to see the new doctor in town. My first patient was a lady from Beaver Creek, Minnesota, and I'll mention her name at this time, Mrs. Marie Rauk. She was #1 on the chart list. My first medical assistant was Arlene Hemme, who had been recommended to me by the Luverne school system. She had just graduated from high school in May of 1954. She was eager to learn and very cooperative, and did a good job. Her beginning wage was $150.00 per month. I taught her how to do lab work, take x-rays, and develop x-rays. She was also the receptionist and the bookkeeper.

In medicine, we have serious times and comedy times, and I'll just mention one event that did occur early in my practice. My x-ray machine did have fluoroscopy on it and there was no other fluoroscopy in Luverne. I had used a fluoroscopy machine with the x-ray machine at General Hospital on occasions so I was familiar with it. This male patient came to see me and complained of some chest pain. He had an irregular heartbeat so I put him on the x-ray machine under the fluoroscope. The assistant turned down the lights and I looked through the fluoroscope to watch the cardiac action and, lo and behold, sparks began to fly across the room. I became panic-stricken for just a moment, thinking that possibly the patient had been electrocuted. Arlene turned on the lights and the patient sat up off the x-ray table and stated, "That's the best x-ray I've ever had!" In fact, he used some expletives to describe how good the x-ray was.

Also, one night I was at the hospital and some people came in with some injuries from a car accident. One lady had a swollen elbow. At that time, we didn't have an x-ray tech., and I had to take my own x-rays with the portable machine. I took the x-rays and then went down into the basement of the hospital to the dark room and developed the x-rays, and they were very poor quality. I really couldn't see too much. I came upstairs and explained to her that we had to retake the x-rays, and they just left the hospital and shook their heads and said, "This is a pretty poor excuse of a place to take care of people."

Well, about one week after I opened my office downtown, a storm came up. I mean a hailstorm, possibly the worst that Luverne has ever seen. This was in the 3rd week of July 1954. Mary and I were invited to go to Sioux Falls to the Town Club and meet her Uncle Herb, her father and mother, and Dr. John and his wife for dinner there. At about 3:00 or 3:30 in the afternoon, this terrible hailstorm hit. It hailed and hailed for approximately 30 minutes, and caused at least a total of $1,000,000.00 of damage within the city limits of Luverne. In the farm country around Luverne, it was devastated. Even cattle and hogs were killed by hail. The hail was heavy and in all sizes and, in fact, 1 or 2 people were injured by hail hitting them in the head.

In my office downtown I heard this terrible racket from the hail and it came right through the sky light. My 1950 Dodge was in a back lot behind Piggly-Wiggly store, and it had huge dents all over it. We closed the office early and as I went home I found out that Mary had had real problems at home. The roof was damaged, the siding on 3 sides of the house were gouged, and all the windows on the north and west sides of the house were beaten in and most of them broken or cracked. There was even glass in the piano in the living room. Mary stated that she hid the boys in the base-ment and the hail had come down so hard it beat the screens into the glass, and then broke the glass. Well, everybody around the town of Luverne was real depressed about the whole situation. But, you know, sometimes good things can come out of bad things. The good things coming from this were that I used the insurance payment on my car to help pay for the x-ray machine, and I let the car sit out in the hot sun and it finally popped the holes out again. We also got a new roof on our house and new siding, as well as new glass windows, and that all went pretty well.

As far as the city of Luverne, it rebounded with lots of people getting work and busy all over town working on houses and so forth. But then we did have some slim pick-ings as far as paying of bills from the farmers because of the severe hailstorm. We did finally make it to Sioux Falls for dinner. When I came to Luverne, they were taking down the Our Savior's Lutheran Church, which Pastor Mundal had been pastor of for 40 years. That church congregation had joined Our Savior's Lutheran Church on the corner of Luverne Street and Freeman Street to form a new congregation, called Our Savior's. This congregation was Emmanuel Lutheran and was served by Pastor Lund.

We joined Our Savior's Lutheran Church at this location. It was a big frame church made of wood. We got involved almost right away with the fact that they would be building a new church. The new church would be called Grace Lutheran and would be built on North Kniss Street or the highway. Also, the hospital building committee had been working real hard. Here I was, just starting in practice, and being approached by 2 organizations, Grace Lutheran Church, and Luverne Hospital, for donations or pledges to both.

The hospital board approached us and Dr. Sherman and Dr. Bofenkamp gave $4,000.00 in pledges, and Doctors Boone, Odland, and Martin all pledged $2,500. To me, that was a lot of money because I was in debt so far. Then I turned around and pledged $2,000.00 to the church. Here I was pledging money I didn't even have! The first few months in practice I ran in the hole, or a very bad negative balance, because of all of the equipment I had to buy. Also, they were making plans with the school board to buy up land and build a new high school. So, although things looked a little dim and depressing to begin with, things were looking up.

About 2 months after I came to Luverne I got a call one morning that an elderly lady was severely injured in the north part of town. I rushed over there real fast and found her lying on the front porch, and her daughter was also present. The woman had a spurting artery. She was bleeding severely from her right arm, and there was blood all over the porch. What had happened was she stumbled and ran her arm through the glass window of the storm door. She had severed her brachial artery right at the antecubital space. At that time, we didn't have an ambulance as such, but the funeral directors were the ambulance people. They rushed over there, too, and we put a tourniquet on her arm and brought her to the hospital. Fortunately, I had some vascular clamps, and we took her to the operating room and I repaired her brachial artery and her arm was saved.

Also, we made farm calls. People just weren't trained at the time to come to the hospital or the office. At night they would call you up and you would make house calls to the farms. This was good and this was bad. The good part is that you did learn where people lived and how they lived, what kind of houses they had, and possibly even their material resources. I would drive to Kenneth on a house call to see a Parkinson's patient, or to Magnolia, and even went to Kanaranzi, Ellsworth, and Hills many a times. I also made calls to farms near Beaver Creek, Minnesota.

Also, because of the lack of facilities here in Luverne, I joined the staff both at McKennen and Sioux Valley Hospitals. I actually was on the active medical staff and surgical staff. I assisted with many operations in both hospitals, but I usually didn't do any surgery myself because the follow-up care was so difficult. However, I would make rounds in Sioux Falls on medical and surgical patients. This, of course, complicated my schedule. By the end of the first calendar year of 1954, I was regularly seeing 30-35 patients in the office, plus all of the house calls and heavy hospital schedule, sometimes seeing about 50 a day.

The fees in those days, well, I'll just give you some examples: Office calls varied between $2.00 and $3.00 a call. Many times I would throw in a penicillin shot for an extra $1.00 - $1.50. Appendectomies were $125.00. Total care for an obstetrical patient was $90.00. This included all the office calls, blood tests, and everything. If they had to have a C-section it would be approximately $175.00. For twins, it would be $200.00 for a C-section. For normal twin delivery, the fee was $125.00. A gallbladder operation would be about $200.00. A vein operation, single side stripping of the saphenous vein, would be about $125.00. So, you can see, even though a large number of people were being seen, the income wasn't that great. Actually, we had a lot of collection problems, too, because 1954-'55 was sort of a down year for the agricultural community in the area. The first year, I took no vacations and had very little time off.

When Christmas came in 1954, Mark was 4 years old and David was 1 year plus 9 months. We had a very nice Christmas and invited people over, that is, the Hermansons, Odlands, Dr. John Hermansons, and Polly Remington and her husband, and several other couples. We enjoyed very much being in Luverne. In fact, on the first New Year of 1955, we had an open house at our home and invited many couples, which was certainly a brave endeavor.

POSTLUDE

What then are we to say about these things? If God is for us, who is against us? He who did not withhold his own Son, but gave him up for all of us, will he not with him also give us everything else? Who will bring charge against God's elect? It is God who justifies. Who is to condemn? It is Christ Jesus, who died, yes, who was raised, who is at the right hand of God, who indeed intercedes for us. Who will separate us from the love of Christ? Will hardship, or distress, or persecution, or famine, or nakedness, or peril, or sword? As it is written, "For your sake we are being killed all day long; we are accounted as sheep to be slaughtered." No, in all these things we are more than conquerors through him who loved us. For I am convinced that neither death, nor life, nor angels, nor rulers, nor things present, nor things to come, nor powers, nor height, nor depth, nor anything else in all creation, will be able to separate us from the love of God in Christ Jesus our Lord.

(Romans 8:31-39)

———>●<———

D r. Donald M. Odland, 69, Luverne physician and surgeon, died at Sioux Valley Hospital Monday evening, October 21, 1996, of an abdominal aneurysm.

Donald Mark Odland was born in Yankton, S.D., October 23, 1926, the son of the Rev. Ole M. Odland and Clara Stensland Odland. He spent his early boyhood in Yankton and attended elementary school there. He moved with his family to Dell Rapids, S.D., in 1937, where he attended high school, graduating with the class of 1944. While in high school, he was active in sports and music.

Shortly after beginning his college studies at University of South Dakota in 1944, he was drafted into the armed forces, and served in the Navy from 1944 to 1946. After being discharged, he attended Augustana College, graduating in 1948. He played football and was a member of the Augustana Symphony.

He married Mary Hermanson, of Dell Rapids, August 1, 1948 at Dell Rapids, and they moved to Milwaukee, where he entered Marquette University School of Medicine. He was graduated with a Doctor of Medicine degree in 1952. Dr. Odland then moved with his family to Minneapolis, where he spent two years of internship at Minneapolis General Hospital.

He and his family moved to Luverne in July, 1954,

where he opened a solo medical practice. The practice expanded over the years, and eventually developed into what is now the Luverne Medical Center, and where he had been on duty part of the forenoon the day of his passing.

During his 42 years in Luverne, he was active in community and church affairs. He was elected coroner and medical examiner of Rock County, a position he still held at the time of his death, with more than 30 years of service to his credit. He served on the Luverne school board for nine years. He belonged to Grace Lutheran Church, and sang with the chancel choir for many years. He had held the office of deacon, and most recently, was a member of the 21st Century Committee. He was currently a member of the Augustana College Board of Regents.

Surviving him are his wife, Mary Odland, of Luverne; four sons and daughters-in-law, Mark and Pat Odland, of Alexandria, David and Sharon Odland, of Marshall, Paul and Jenny Odland, of Alexandria, and Steve Odland of Woodbury; one daughter, Debbie Odland, of Woodbury; and nine grandchildren, Mark Patrick, Matthew, Anthony, Kristoffer, Laura, Eric, Ryan, Will, Wade, and a 10th grandchild due in October, 2003.

LAMPLIGHTER

He has taken his bright candle and is gone
Into another room I cannot find,
Buy anyone can tell where he has been
By all the little lights he leaves behind.

Printed in the United States
1512200001B/374